JUN FAN JEET KUNE DO
THE TEXTBOOK

by Chris Kent & Tim Tackett

EMPIRE BOOK/AWP LLC
Los Angeles, CA.

DISCLAIMER

Please note that the author and publisher of this book are NOT RESPONSIBLE in any manner whatsoever for any injury that may result from practicing the techniques and/or following the instructions given within. Since the physical activities described herein may be too strenuous in nature for some readers to engage in safely, it is essential that a physician be consulted prior to training.

Revised Edition published in 2025 by AWP LLC/Empire Books. Copyright (c) 2025 by AWP LLC/Empire Books/Chris Kent/Tim Tackett.

All rights reserved. No part of this publication may be reproduced or utilized in any form or by any means, electronic or mechanical, including photo- copying, recording, or by any information storage and retrieval system, without prior written permission from AWP LLC/Empire Books.

Revised edition Library of Congress Catalog Number:
ISBN-13: 978-1-949753-90-5
25 24 23 22 21 20 19 18 17 16 15 14 13 12
Library of Congress Cataloging-in-Publication Data
Jun Fan Jeet Kune Do - The Textbook by Chris Kent and Tim Tackett -- ed. p. cm.
ISBN 978-1-949753-90-5 (pbk. : alk. paper) 1. Martial arts-- philosophy. 3. Large type books. I. Title. GV1114.3.F719 20713261.815'3--dc22
20060101924

Printed in the United States of America.

DEDICATION

To my wife Gerry,
for her support
throughout the years.
—*Tim*

To my wife Leslie,
for her encouragement
and support,
perseverance and love.
—*Chris*

ACKNOWLEDGEMENTS

Thanks to **Cass Magda** (Full Instructor-Jun Fan), **Hal Faulkner** (Associate Instructor-Jun Fan), and to Jun Fan Apprentice Instructors **Dennis Blue, Keith Jung,** and **Mark Sanden,** for their assistance in the photographs.

Special thanks to **Dr. Michael Yessis, Ph.D.,** and **Jerry Robinson** (Health for Life), for their technical expertise and assistance.

To the students we train, for aiding in our martial arts growth.

To **Dan Inosanto,** our martial arts mentor.

And to our JKD brothers.

Dan Inosanto

Hal Faulkner Book participants: Cass Magda, Chris Kent, Dennis Blue, Keith Jung and Tim Tackett. Mark Sanden

DISCLAIMER: Although both Unique Publications and the authors of this martial arts book have taken great care to ensure the authenticity of the information and techniques contained herein, we are not responsible, in whole are in part, for an injury which may occur to the reader by following the instructions in this publication.

CONTENTS

ABOUT THE AUTHORS 6
INTRODUCTION 10
PREFACE 11
JUN FAN GUNG FU 12
WHAT IS JEET KUNE DO? 13
BASIC ELEMENT OF ATTACK 16
HAND IMMOBILIZATION AND ENERGY DRILLS 31
ENERGY/SENSITIVITY TRAINING 51
DISTANCE AND MOBILITY 72
ATTACK 84
COUNTERATTACK 112
TIMING AND RHYTHM 125
ESSENTIAL QUALITIES 137
TACTICS AND STRATEGY 149
TRAINING METHODOLOGY 156
COMPREHENDING THE TRUE NATURE OF JKD 162
THE JKD "TRAINING PYRAMID" 167
GLOSSARY OF JUN FAN TERMINOLOGY 168
APPENDIX 169

ABOUT THE AUTHORS

CHRIS KENT

With over 50 years of experience, Chris Kent is widely acknowledged as one of the world's foremost authorities on Jeet Kune Do and has gained international recognition for his knowledge and leadership in perpetuating the art, training methods, and philosophy developed by the legendary Bruce Lee. Chris is considered one of the few individuals in the world having total comprehension of all facets of Lee's martial art.

In 1973, Chris became the youngest and final member admitted into Dan Inosanto's now fabled "Backyard JKD" group during Bruce Lee's lifetime. He studied with and assisted Inosanto for over 13 years, mastering his skills and traveling extensively both nationally and internationally while serving as Inosanto's personal assistant for seminars and public exhibitions. In 1982, Chris became one of the first students to be awarded the prestigious title of Full Instructor under Inosanto.

In the over five decades that he has been intimately involved in Jeet Kune Do, while holding true to the original spirt and vision with which Bruce Lee developed Jeet Kune Do, Kent has performed extensive research into the foundations of the art from a technical, philosophical, and spiritual perspective, as well as educating himself in the fields of exercise physiology, kinesiology, and human performance. This commitment to continuous improvement has made him one of the most sought-after instructors of Jeet Kune Do and its applications. As a teacher and professional consultant, Kent has traveled the world, teaching and sharing the benefit of his expertise in Jeet Kune Do with thousands of people.

Chris' friendship and affiliation with Lee's family, personal assistants, students, and friends allows him to hold a unique position in the JKD world – a direct pipeline to Bruce Lee's art and philosophy. According to Linda Lee Cadwell (Bruce Lee's wife) -- "I am in awe of the growth I have witnessed in my friend Chris Kent. I have known Chris for close to 50 years from the time he first took up the practice of Bruce Lee's way of martial arts, Jeet Kune Do. Chris not only learned the martial aspect of Bruce's teachings but also his methods of self-reflection as a goal to personal development".

Possessing an exuberant teaching style as well as an uncanny ability to transfer knowledge to students and teachers alike, Chris is a teacher par excellence, whose innovative teaching and training methods help students to maximize their physical skills and achieve their full potential as martial artists. As a teaching consultant, Chris shares his passion for Jeet Kune Do with other instructors, who, in turn, share the art and philosophy with their students, Chris has worked in a consultant capacity and collaborated with numerous JKD instructors and schools, assisting them regarding such things as training protocols, teaching methodology, and training curriculum design.

Recognized for his knowledge and expertise and known as a "teacher of teachers"; Chris' goal is to help develop instructors who are equally passionate about JKD, and who possess the ability to convey their knowledge to the highest degree through movement and language.

Driven by a passion and desire to share authentic knowledge and insights regarding Jeet Kune Do, Chris is an accomplished writer and author. In addition to the books he has authored/co-authored on Jeet Kune Do, he has both written and for and appeared in countless martial art publications both nationally and internationally, including Inside Kung Fu, Black Belt, Martial Arts Masters, Budo International, Combat, Martial Arts Illustrated, and Bruce Lee Mania. Seeking to share his knowledge in all forms of media Chris wrote and produced three series of training DVDs which remain the standard of the industry.

Chris is not only one of the world's foremost authorities and experts on Bruce Lee's martial art training process, but also on his philosophy of self-actualization and personal liberation. His recent book, "LIBERATE YOURSELF! – How to Think Like Bruce Lee" and its accompanying workbook detail how individuals can apply the philosophical tenets of self-actualization utilized by Bruce Lee to their own lives. As a consultant and personal development specialist, Chris has helped countless individuals including celebrities, professional athletes, and corporate executives achieve liberation of body, mind, and spirit so that they can attain their goals and live a rich and rewarding life.

An inspiring and effective communicator, Chris has been a featured guest speaker on numerous radio talk programs, podcasts, and at public events, discussing not only Bruce Lee and his art and philosophy of Jeet Kune Do, but also how the much broader application of the principles can enhance an individual's personal and professional life. In 2023 he was a featured speaker at TEDx Youngstown "Life Happens."

In addition to his expertise in Jeet Kune Do, Chris also holds the title of Full Instructor in the Filipino martial arts of Kali-Escrima under Inosanto; and in 1976 was awarded the title of "Escrimador". In 1988 Chris received a Moniteur certificate (Teaching credential), Silver Glove (Technical) and Bronze Glove (Competition) rankings in the French Kickboxing sport of Boxe Francaise-Savate from the French Federation.

As part of his belief in giving back to the community, Chris created "S.A.V.E." (Safety Against Violence Education) a personal safety awareness training program which teaches personal safety education and self-protection skills to women and children as well as businesses and corporations.

In 1996, Chris was a one of the co-founders of "The Bruce Lee Educational Foundation." For five years he served as a member of the Board of Directors, then moved to an advisory position to the re-established "Bruce Lee Foundation."

In Hollywood, Chris martial art skills led to stunt work, serving as a technical advisor and fight action choreographer for both television and feature films. "Miami Vice" creator/producer Anthony Yerkovich, "Pink Panther" film director/producer Blake Edwards, and The Incredible Hulk, Lou Ferrigno are among the elite Hollywood clientele who sought Mr. Kent out for his technical assistance and training expertise.

Working in the field of professional sports, Chris served as a training consultant to professional sports teams including the San Francisco 49ers. He has also worked with many law enforcement personnel and has been extensively involved in the field of executive security for the entertainment industry, including such events as The Golden Globe Awards and American Film Institute Special Tributes. For three years after its opening, Chris served as Director of Security for Santa Monica's "Buffalo Club", an exclusive, private supper-club catering to high-profile members of Hollywood's entertainment industry.

Social media platforms:

Website: https://ckjkd.com
Facebook: https://www.facebook.com/ckjkd
Pinterest: https://www.pinterest.com/jkd4life/
YouTube: https://www.youtube.com/@chriskentjeetkunedo123
https://www.youtube.com/@chriskentjkd_dpl
https://www.youtube.com/@ChrisKent-ThinkLikeBruceLee
Instagram: https://www.instagram.com/ck_jkd_dpl/

ABOUT THE AUTHORS

TIM TACKETT

While in the U.S.A.F., Sifu Tackett was stationed in Taiwan for almost three years. While he was there, he studied Kuo Shu (Kung Fu). His wife was working as a teacher at the Taipei American School during the day, and he was working in the evening at the Shu Lin Kuo Air Force Station. Since he had his days free, he started to look for something to occupy his time. One of his friends recommended that he take up martial arts. He ended up training six hours a day, six days a week. While in Taiwan, he studied two types of Hsing-I, Tai Chi, Northern and Southern Shaolin, White Crane, and Monkey Boxing. After his discharge from the Air Force, he continued working on his college degree. Since he had a wife and two children to support, he opened a full-time Kung Fu school in Redlands, California, while starting as a junior at the University of California, Riverside campus, in 1966.

In 1967, he saw Bruce Lee demonstrate JKD at Ed Parker's tournament in Long Beach, CA, and wanted to start studying with him right on the spot. However, he soon realized that he would not have enough time until after he finished college. In 1968, he started a Master of Fine Arts program at UCR and no longer had time to teach martial arts full-time. So he closed down his school and rented a hall in Redlands two nights a week, where he taught what he called "Chinese Karate," as hardly anyone had heard of "Kung Fu," let alone "Kuo Shu."

In 1970, he received his M.F.A. and began teaching drama in high school. Soon after, his first student, Bob Chapman, and he, on the recommendation of Dan Lee, sought out Dan Inosanto. Dan had opened a backyard Jeet Kune Do school after Bruce Lee closed his Los Angeles Chinatown school shortly before moving to Hong Kong to star in movies. Both men felt privileged to be accepted into Dan Inosanto's backyard class. The class consisted of about 10 students, and Sifu Tackett got to meet for the first time such JKD luminaries as Bob Bremer, Dan Lee, Richard Bustillo, Jerry Poteet, and Pete Jacobs. Later, Chris Kent, Ted Lucaylucay, and Jeff Imada joined the private group of students.

In 1973, Dan Inosanto honored Tackett with the rank of "Senior First," and he was given permission to have a small Jeet Kune Do group. In Dan's backyard school, it was always stressed that JKD was something special. There were certain techniques that Bruce Lee did not want given out outside of what we all felt was a small and special group. Dan told us that Bruce said, "If knowledge is power, then why pass it out indiscriminately?"

Like many Jeet Kune Do students, Tackett received supplemental training in Western boxing, Thai boxing, wrestling, and Wing Chun. He has been described by Dan Inosanto as "one of the most knowledgeable JKD instructors in the world."

Sifu Tackett taught the principles of JKD and used them as tools to examine the martial arts he had learned up to that point. He found that much of what he had been teaching previously was not very efficient. Since he didn't want to teach JKD openly, he closed the school and moved the senior group to his garage, where he started the famous "JKD Wed Night" group.

These are the three core concepts of the JKD Wednesday Night Group as described by Tim Tackett. *The Core Principle is "Maintaining and Utilizing Distance". "In order to do that one must be able to use distance for both attack and defense. Too many people prioritize one or the other and end up unbalanced. Instead, people should train as if they are both attacking and defending from the "Fighting Measure" using proper footwork."*

The first core principle is the "Leg Obstruction". "The primary defensive and offensive attack is the leg obstruction. Most of the time, you will be able to use the leg obstruction defensively. It is important to be able to use leg obstruction offensively as well as one may need to strike first. The main reason to practice the leg obstruction is to use it against an opponent that practices intercepting as their main defense. When attacking with the leg obstruction, you may enter based on the opponent's movement patterns or telegraphed strikes. From this point, you can trap or strike depending on the opponent's stance."

The second core principle is the "Finger Jab Drill". "This drill is one of the most important and foundational drills. Its goal is to reduce and eliminate the telegraphing of strikes. In this drill, one partner will stand with their hands raised to block the other partner's incoming finger jab. The partner jabbing should aim to touch the forehead of their partner without the partner parrying their strike. If the blocking partner is able to parry their strike, they should announce what prompted their parry so the partner can aim to eliminate the movement that caused them to block. It is essential to practice all drills with varying partners in groups of two to learn to adapt to different movement patterns. Both partners will benefit as the attacker eliminates the preparation and the parry partner will learn to notice preparation. Once you master this drill, you can hit without intention."

Finally the third core principle is the "Time Commitment Theory." "This was taken directly from Bruce Lee's notes and is one of the key teachings of our group. The theory states that any type of technique requires a certain amount of time. For example, a straight punch would include both the forward and backward motion of the punch as well as the recovery time to return to a proper stance. The more time a certain movement takes, the more vulnerable one is to counterattacks. One must weigh the options and make smart decisions with the "Time Commitment Theory" in mind. A combination of varying types of punches and kicks should be trained. The "Time Commitment Theory" is one of the best tools one has to analyze their techniques.

Social media platforms:

Website: https://jkdwednite.com
Facebook: https://www.facebook.com/TimTackettJKD
Instagram: www.instagram.com/jkdwng

INTRODUCTION

Even today, nearly forty years after our second book "Jun Fan/Jeet Kune Do - The Textbook" was originally published, it's still recognized by many around the world as one of the best books written about Bruce Lee's art and philosophy of Jeet Kune Do. At the time it was published it quickly received recognition as the best book dealing with the subject on a technical level.

As part of our research for the book, Tim and I met personally with Michael Yessis Ph.D., a professor of physical education at California State University Fullerton, and a training and technique consultant to several American Olympic, professional, and amateur sports teams, to talk to him in-depth about sports training methodology. At the time, Yessis was one of the leading authorities on Soviet sports training methodology and author of Secrets of Soviet Sports Fitness and Training. Much of the material dealing with how to improve essential qualities such as speed and power are the result of that interview.

In addition to my teaching, inspired by Bruce Lee's depth and breadth of research and investigation, I personally spent a great deal of time researching such things as kinesiology, exercise physiology, sports training, etc., as I was highly interested in the subject of human performance. As I built my research library, I was fortunate enough to find several books written in English on the subject of sports training that were published in Russia and East Germany, and incredibly hard to get hold of, each which contained a wealth of training information that I felt could be applied to the study and practice of JKD.

At the same time, Tim, working with original Chinatown Bruce Lee student Bob Bremer, friend Bert Poe, and a small, tight-knit group of diehard students and instructors which met at his home and was known as the "Wednesday Night Group", was deeply immersed in conducting his own research and investigation regarding Jeet Kune Do.

As with our first book, "Jeet Kune Do Kickboxing", each of us wrote what we felt should be included in the book on our own, then afterward came together to flesh out and finalize what eventually ended up being in it. Our approach worked amazingly well, and the result speaks for itself.

And as I stated in the new Introduction for JKD Kickboxing, the martial art world has grown and changed a great deal since The Textbook was originally published. Advancements in training methodology, equipment, nutrition, etc., have helped martial artists reach new levels of performance. The explosive growth of what is known as 'mixed martial arts,' both as a combative sport and as self-defense has led (or in some cases forced) people to look at martial arts from a new perspective. And it's an indisputable fact that Bruce Lee and his revolutionary approach to martial art training served as a catalyst for many of these changes.

Tim and I wrote "Jun Fan /Jeet Kune Do - The Textbook", not as a technical how-to manual for Jeet Kune Do, but to share with people the overall picture of Bruce Lee's method of self-discovery, help them explore the qualities and combative motions that make one's tools work as efficiently and effectively as possible, and enhance their personal performance. If it does that for you, we will both be very happy.

In the Spirit of JKD,

Chris Kent and Tim Tackett

PREFACE

The *Tao of Jeet Kune Do* is a compilation of several volumes of written notes and observations that Bruce Lee felt had validity in whatever he wanted to achieve for himself. These notes were drawn from many sources—boxing, fencing, gung fu systems, etc. The sources were both ancient and modern. Many pages of the original volumes were headlined with a single question related to some aspect of fighting or training, and blank underneath. Questions such as "What is my counter to a left stancer's front snapping kick?" The page was left blank in order to be filled in at some later time, possibly after more research and investigation. To reiterate, they were for himself.

The reason for writing this book is a simple one. In the seeking by many of the eclecticism so freely labeled and attached to Jeet Kune Do, the foundations from which Lee evolved his personal fighting theories and philosophies have been overshadowed. Many of these foundations existed before Bruce and will still continue to exist long after most of us are gone.

So the objective of this book is to expose the reader to the various aspects of the Jun Fan Martial Arts and allow them to see the overall picture. While this book does show certain techniques in various chapters, that is not what it is about. Many books have been written about the techniques of martial arts. They deal with the basic tools of combat such as punching, kicking, and blocking. This "how to" however is not enough to create a successful fighter.

One may know how to punch and even have adequate power, but without the proper timing the punch will never score. One may know how to kick, but without a feeling for the proper distance the kick will never land. One may be able to punch and kick in combination but without the proper visual awareness he may not see the correct opening when it occurs. And for a counter to work you need timing, rhythm and the proper distance.

The purpose of this book is to explore those qualities and combative motions that make the tools work. It is qualities such as balance, precision, speed, awareness, distance, and attitude that make the tools work. Many fighters come by these qualities naturally. They are born with good speed, fantastic coordination, and superior balance. In many ways these qualities can never be taught but can only be improved upon. Other qualities such as endurance, power, and good form can be cultivated to a high level transcending the natural abilities one was born with. Some qualities such as timing, awareness, and distance can be learned through ring experience or actual combat. It is the cultivation of these qualities that makes a seasoned fighter. To learn only from fighting is the survival of the fittest theory of learning. If you fight enough and survive you will cultivate these qualities. Surely there is a way to achieve these qualities without getting your brains bashed in. Do you have to fight to learn to fight?

Bruce Lee believed that you could cultivate these qualities through drilling. In his school as you improved your skills the drills became more and more complex until you were all-out sparring even against two or more opponents.

Thus in Jun Fan/JKD training there is a natural progression that tries to go beyond the old progressive one-step sparring to all-out sparring with nothing in between. It is this "in between" that this book concerns itself with. As Bruce Lee once wrote, "The 'how to' is important but to be successful necessitates the 'why' and 'when'." This book is about the "why" and the "when" as well as the "how to."

The Jun Fan System

---Sticking to the Nucleus

---Liberation from the Nucleus

---Returning to the Original Freedom

JUN FAN GUNG FU

On March 27, 1981, Jun Fan Gung Fu/Jeet Kune was inducted into the Kuoshu Federation of the Republic of China, making it a legitimate and recognized martial art such as Tai Chi, etc. (It is a recognized art, not a style.)

In this there are four levels:

1. ELDERS—Direct descendants of Bruce Lee (Dan Inosanto, Taky Kimura, etc.).

2. PAI SHO—Direct descendants of elders (Chris Kent, Tim Tackett, Ted Lucaylucay, Cass Magda, etc.).

3. AFFILIATES—Those who are trained by the above but not necessarily on a full-time regular basis. (People such as Rick Faye, Dick Harrell, etc.)

4. PARTICIPANTS AND LIAISONS—People not affiliated with Jun Fan but who aid in its perpetuation or who act as advisors. (People such as Lucky Lucaylucay, Bert Poe.)

Jun Fan is the foundation from which Jeet Kune Do eventually evolved. It is what Bruce Lee taught and referred to as his Martial Way before the term Jeet Kune Do came into existence. If JKD is a way of thinking, training, researching, and experimenting, the Jun Fan Martial Arts are a primary vehicle to get you there.

JUN FAN TRAINING CONSISTS OF:
1. Punching and striking techniques.
2. Kicking and kneeing techniques.
3. Joint locking techniques.
4. Choking and strangling techniques.
5. Grappling, throwing, takedown, and sweeping techniques.

JUN FAN GUNG FU CONSISTS OF:
Wing Chun (Jun Fan)
Gung Fu (Jun Fan)
Western boxing (Jun Fan)
Kickboxing (Jun Fan)
Chin na
Jun Fan weaponry

(In 1967 these became Jeet Kune Do. What JKD is will be explored in the next chapter.)

Each of the above aspects of the Jun Fan Martial Arts, while being a separate entity, is also part of the 'whole' and must be able to be linked with all of the other aspects. The linking of the various facets is one of the most important aspects of the total Jun Fan program, and one of which a tremendous amount of training is aimed.

A point should be made about the term "modified." Modifications were never made just for the sake of change, or simply because something looked pretty or better. Modification in Jun Fan evolved gradually, through a constant process of trial and error, and experimentation. A technique was modified only because it did not theoretically accomplish what Bruce felt it should, and nothing was changed unless a genuine improvement could be demonstrated.

And Jun Fan is still evolving. Throughout the years since Lee's death, training methods from other martial arts such as Muay Thai, Savate, Pentjak Silat, etc., have been synthesized into the Jun Fan curriculum in order to improve constantly.

The following excerpts are from an article written for *Inside Kung Fu* magazine by Dan Inosanto.

"To Bruce Lee, martial art knowledge and martial arts learning were two separate realities. According to Lee, martial art knowledge is of the past and martial art learning is in the present."

"The traditional training methods and the traditional techniques along with the classic styles and the classic martial arts writings provide us a link to the wisdom and knowledge of the early pioneering practitioners and founders of the martial arts."

"The knowledge and wisdom of these founders are in and of themselves just a product, and like any product it must change with the times or the environment."

"To quote Bruce Lee, 'To be bound by traditional martial art style or styles is the way of the mindless, enslaved martial artist, but to be inspired by the traditional martial art and to achieve further heights is the way of genius.'"

WHAT IS JEET KUNE DO?

Ever since the tragic and untimely death of Bruce Lee there has been a controversy about just what Jeet Kune Do is. If you ask 10 different Bruce Lee students you are likely to get 10 different, although similar, answers. These definitions tend to frustrate editors of martial arts magazines who look for neatly packaged answers to serve their reading public.

After Bruce's death there was never any intention to commercialize JKD. There was no thought to having seminars on JKD or of writing books on the subject. But it wasn't too long after Lee's death before we noticed Jeet Kune Do schools springing up around the world. The one thing these spurious schools had in common was that what they taught had little to do with JKD. One of the main reasons for giving JKD seminars was to educate the public as to what authentic JKD really was. But still there was some confusion because some of us used the words Jeet Kune Do, or Jeet Kune Do concepts, while others preferred to use the term Jun Fan Gung Fu.

Because of this, many questions about JKD remain. The questions about JKD are many and varied. For example: What is Jeet Kune Do? Was it merely Bruce Lee's expression of himself in combat? Is it a style? Is it a system? Is it a process? Is it a product? Can it be taught? And is it merely an amalgamation of other martial arts techniques?

Much of this confusion stems from the use of the words Jun Fan Gung Fu and Jeet Kune Do. When we were in Dan Inosanto's backyard school in the early 1970s and Bruce was still alive, we were learning Jeet Kune Do at the Jun Fan Gung Fu Institute. While the word institute makes this sound like a large school, in reality it consisted of about 12 students, most of whom had black belts in various traditional martial arts. It is hard to remember that before Bruce, if you trained in a martial art, you were trained in a traditional martial art. It was Bruce Lee's genius that helped us break the shackles of a particular mind-set of a style or system.

What did we learn there? It is easier to start off with what we did not learn. We did not learn a particular style or system of martial arts there. In the episode of the television show *Longstreet* entitled "Jeet Kune Do," the leading character asks Bruce to teach him. The character Bruce plays replies, "I don't believe in system or method and without system or method, what's to teach?" Later, Bruce's character relents and starts to teach Longstreet. He tells Longstreet, "To reach me you must move to me, and I will intercept your movement." This idea of intercepting movement is outside of a particular style or method. It is a concept that is not exclusive to a particular style or method. For example, this concept can be seen in the stop hit of Western fencing, but it doesn't belong only to that method. Bruce asked himself, "If I don't have a sword how can I use this concept?" His answer was a stroke of genius. He put his strong hand forward as a fencer does. Then he added the stance and the lead step from Western boxing, and he combined those concepts with the Wing Chun vertical punch. He then named his study of combat after this concept and called it Jeet Kune Do or the way of the intercepting fist. But this was merely a name and he said not to "fuss over it." If you intercept a movement toward you with a kick, this is called Jeet Kune Tek or the way of the intercepting kick. So we can see that the name Jeet Kune Do does not really define what the art is.

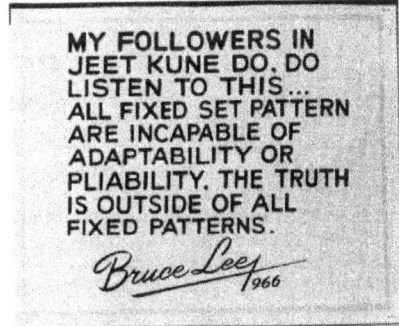

What we were learning in Dan Inosanto's backyard was not a style or system, for Bruce Lee taught that "True observation begins when devoid of set patterns, and freedom of expression occurs when one is beyond styles, method, system and organizations." Another time he wrote, "Jeet Kune Do is training and discipline toward the ultimate reality in combat. The ultimate reality is the returning to one's primary freedom which is simple, direct, and non-classical." The key word in both quotes is freedom. To truly express, you can not be bound to a particular style, system or method

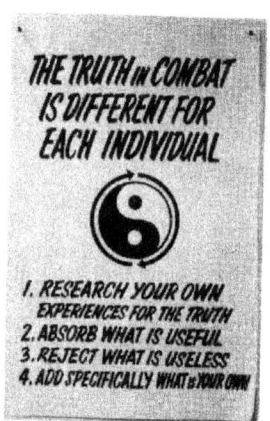

because any style, system, or method are by their very nature fixed, set patterns which Bruce said are incapable of adaptability or pliability. The TRUTH is indeed always "outside of all fixed patterns." Thus a style or system can only be by its very nature a partial truth. This does not mean that a particular style is not good or is not efficient. It is quite possible that the best Muay Thai boxer in the world could defeat any other fighter in the world in the ring. Let's say that a great Thai boxer defeats a great Jiu Jitsu man. Does that make Thai boxing better than Jiu Jitsu? No! It simply means that that particular Thai fighter was able to keep the Jiu Jitsu man within the range that negated what the Jiu Jitsu man is efficient in. And if the Jiu Jitsu man is able to bridge the gap, throw the Thai boxer to the ground, and choke him out, does that mean Jiu Jitsu is better than Thai boxing? Of course not. What Bruce was trying to get at is primary freedom in which one utilizes "all ways and is bound by none." Is it not better to learn the round kick, knees, and elbows of Thai boxing as well as Jiu Jitsu throws and chokes so that you can fit into all ranges of combat?

Let's say a person learns as many different martial arts as possible. He may study Western boxing, Wing Chun, Kali, Savate, Muay Thai boxing, Jiu Jitsu, and Pentjak Silat. Let's say he takes what works for him from these various styles. Is what he ends up with Jeet Kune Do? Not necessarily. JKD is more than just an eclectic martial art. It is more than just grabbing techniques from various martial arts. It is more than an accumulation of techniques. There must be a common thread. In fact JKD can be partially defined as a search for the common thread. There must be a common thread, an analysis, and a concept of what will work for you. Let's discuss the idea of a common thread first.

Suppose a karate black belt goes to a Thai boxing seminar and learns the mechanics of the Thai boxing round kick, which in our experience is one of the most, if not the most, powerful kicks. To add that kick to his repertoire, the karate man must make a radical change in his stance. To perform the Thai round kick most efficiently it must be done from the Thai kicking stance which is much narrower than a karate stance. If the karate man keeps his karate stance and does a Thai round kick, he will have a stronger kick than his roundhouse kick, but the kick will be too slow compared to the Thai's to be really efficient. The karate man must also learn not to focus his kick but rather kick through the target. So to add the Thai kick, the karate man must in a sense, unlearn karate.

The Thai boxer has two basic stances. At kicking range he uses the narrow kick stance. In hand range he will shift to a stance that is the same as a Western boxing stance since punching is more efficient from that stance. The Thai boxer is very adept at moving from one stance to the other. Since the JKD man already has trained the boxing stance it is much easier for him to go into the kicking stance than it is for the traditional karate man. And since the JKD man has already learned not to focus his kicks, it is easier to learn the mechanics of the Thai round kick.

So some of the common threads between JKD and Muay Thai are the boxing stance and the concept of not focusing your kick. And if the JKD man has studied Kali, as most of us have, then even more common threads exist because of Kali's emphasis on knee and elbow attacks. Without these common threads you may end up with two separate elements like copper and zinc. With a common thread copper and zinc can come together to form the alloy, brass. With brass we can no longer see copper and zinc even though we know they are still there.

The second principle of JKD is analysis. This analysis has three basic parts. The first is analysis of a particular technique. The best way to analyze is to ask questions, not of your teacher but of yourself. Some of these questions are as follows: What are the strengths of this technique? What are the weaknesses? How can I adapt this technique to fit me? At what range is it most effective? At what range is it least effective? What is the best way to maintain the most effective range? If it is a close range technique, then what is the best way to bridge the gap? Is it best used as an entry, a follow-up, or as a finishing technique? How does environment (for example, terrain) affect this technique? What is the best way to counter it? What is the best way to avoid a counter? And where does distance and timing fit in?

The second thing to analyze is your opponent. Some of the questions to ask are as follows: What particular technique will be most effective? What will be the least? What range will be most effective? If you weigh 160 pounds and your opponent weighs 290 pounds and looks like he can bench press a truck, it is probably not a good idea to try to throw him to the ground and arm lock him. It may be better to try and keep your distance and finger jab his eyes. The main problem that can occur is if you're bound to a particular style or range of combat and lack the ability to adjust to your opponent's strengths and weaknesses. This can occur if you are "just" a boxer, or "just" a wrestler, or "just" a kicker. A guiding principle of JKD is to learn to fit in with all styles and be bound by none, so you can fit in with any opponent. As Bruce Lee said, "To learn the principle, abide with the principle, and dissolve the principle. In short, to enter a mold without being caged in it, and to obey the principles without being bound by them." When you can do this, you will have achieved primary freedom. But before you can do that you must first know yourself.

JKD is a problem-solving art that Dan Inosanto says, "is highly individualized. Therefore, it has to be different for each person. Like, a tiger can not fight like an eagle, and an eagle can not fight like a tiger. So you have to find out what your pluses and minuses are and go from there." This is where self-analysis comes in.

Any fighter will have a preference which comes from a natural tendency. Some will be very fast on their feet and will prefer to stay at long range. Some will be very strong and prefer to close the gap quickly to better utilize their strength. It is the same thing in football. Some people are natural running backs while some are natural linemen. In JKD we would never try to turn a lineman into a running back. If a student comes to us and is already proficient as a wrestler, we will not try and make a long range fighter out of him. We will rather try and make his wrestling more efficient. But at the same time he will be trained to be as proficient as possible in the other ranges of combat so he can fit into any environment. But he would specialize in the close range arts.

A Jun Fan/JKD concept school can be equated to a university. Just as a student in a university may major in history and have a broad knowledge, he is also expected to have at least a basic knowledge of other subjects. In graduate school he is expected to focus on one era of history. And when he is working for his Ph.D. he has narrowed his education to one specific topic. At this point he doesn't have a teacher; he has an advisor. He is in effect his own teacher having a breath of knowledge to draw upon.

This is not to say that the Jun Fan student's knowledge gets narrower and narrower as he progresses. The analogy is that the student is given a broad education at the beginning level. At the same time he is encouraged to follow his natural tendencies and to think for himself. He is encouraged to express himself instead of his teacher. And at the postgraduate or JKD level he is truly expressing himself.

Since no teacher can teach a student at this level, in a sense JKD can not be taught. As Bruce Lee said, "The teacher is only the finger pointing the way." Or as Kahlil Gibran so eloquently expressed it in his classic *The Prophet*, "No man can reveal to you aught but that which already lies half asleep in the dawning of your knowledge. The teacher who walks in the shadow of the temple, among his followers, gives not of his wisdom but rather of his faith and his lovingness. If he is indeed wise he does not bid you enter the house of his wisdom, but rather leads you to the threshold of your own mind."

We can remember Dan Inosanto telling us that going to a martial arts teacher and learning a technique is like going to a man every day for a fish. After a while you become dependent on the man who gives you the fish. We should instead teach the student to fish for himself.

To sum it all up, JKD can not be taught since individual expression can not be taught. What can and is taught are the principles and concepts that lead the student to his liberation from style and system. The guideposts can be called Jun Fan or JKD concepts which are the path towards the student's own journey of self-discovery. We hope this book will help start your journey.

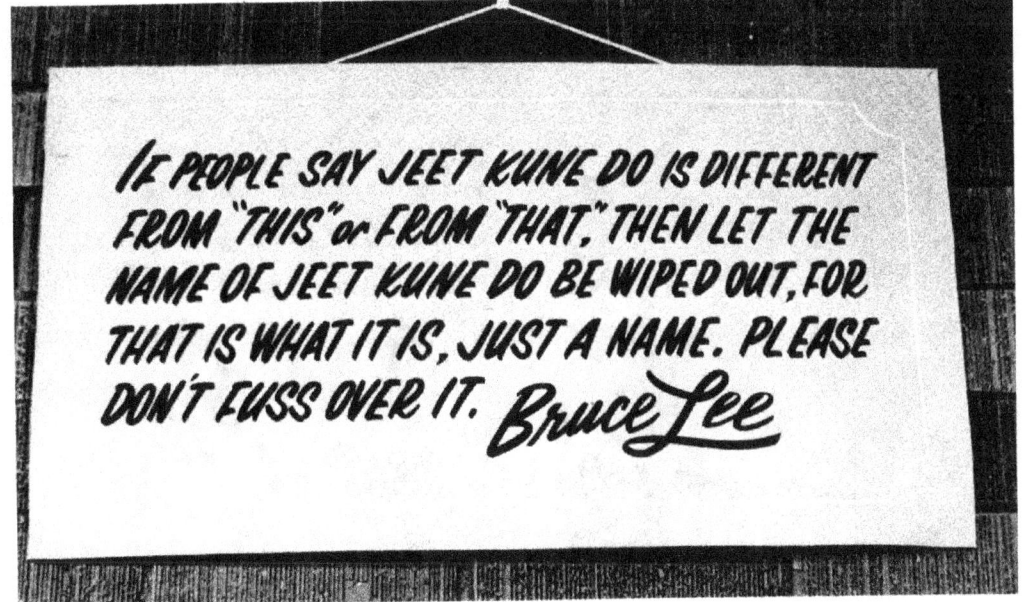

BASIC ELEMENT OF ATTACK

This chapter deals with the basic elements of Jun Fan such as on-guard positioning, weapons of attack, target zones, and various types of on-guard positions one may encounter.

The on-guard position is the platform from which your attack is launched, the various striking weapons are the "tools of the trade," and the opponent's preparatory position may designate which target zones are initially open to attack.

ON-GUARD POSITIONING

The Small Phasic Bent Knee Position (Bai Jong) is a ready position which offers you the ability to move, to hold, to organize yourself around your own physical center. Such a ready position should:

1. Be a neutral, non-committed position.
2. Enable you to move any direction rapidly and with complete ease.
3. Allow you to defend attacks from any angle.
4. Be balanced so that you can "explode" with your attack the instant an opening occurs.
5. Be constantly shifting and adjusting in relationship to the opponent.

The lead hand should be in constant small motion and shifts sometimes from a high to middle position to constantly threaten and confuse the opponent. The rear guarding hand likewise should shift around depending upon the situation but still protects the head. It may be:

Alongside the chin.

Directly in front of chin.

On the opposite side of face.

In the on-guard position, the area to be protected by the hands can be defined by imagining a box from the top of the head to groin level, and down each side of the body.

This area can be defined as your personal airspace, whereas the surrounding area is international airspace. Attacks should be prevented from entering your perimeters. Attacks lower than groin level are handled with either distance, angulation or countering with your own leg.

TARGET ZONES

Your opponent's body is divided into three levels—High (head), Middle (shoulder to groin), and Low (legs), and into two sides—inside and outside.

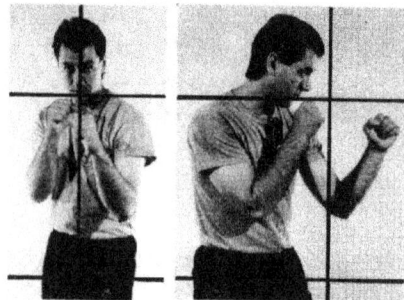

You also have a front sector and a rear sector.

The positioning of your opponent's body may affect which target or sectors are open for attack.

The opponent may be:

3/4 turn   Straight sideways   Full on facing

The following are several examples of various types of on-guard positions you may encounter:

Tight compact guard, open guard, one hand up—one down.

Peek-a-boo guard, crouching position, Muay Thai guard.

Look at each example and notice what levels or sectors are open to attack and which ones only appear to be open to draw your attack.

WEAPONS

In Jun Fan the primary purpose is striking, kicking, and applying bodily force. The various weapons used to accomplish this are:

(A) FOOT

The toes

Ball of foot

Instep

Bottom of foot

Side (in/out)

Heel

Which area of the foot you use to kick with depends upon: (a) whether or not you are wearing shoes; (b) the type of kick; and (c) the target area you are kicking.

(B) SHIN Front/Rear

(C) KNEE Front/Rear

Upward

Inward

Downward

(D) HAND

Vertical punch

In Wing Chun the vertical punch is used to keep the elbow in and cut across the opponent's arm.

18

Horizontal punch

3/4 turn

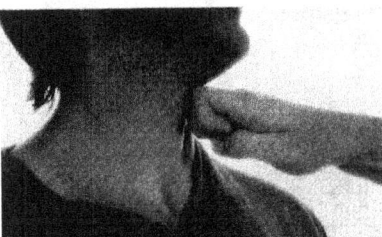
Knuckle fist

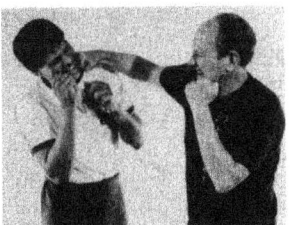
Horizontal hook

Vertical hook

Some boxing instructors teach the horizontal hook while others stress the vertical hook. Experiment to see which one works for you.

Backfist

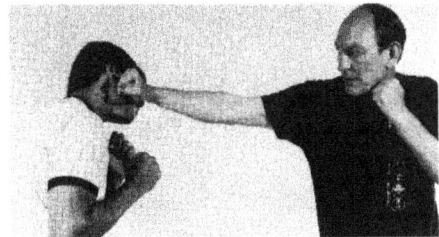

While most martial artists teach the backfist with the knuckles, we feel this is dangerous in combat because if your opponent lowers his head, the chances are you could break your hand.

PALM STRIKES

Jao sao palm

We feel the jao sao palm is better than the traditional ridge hand for the following reasons:

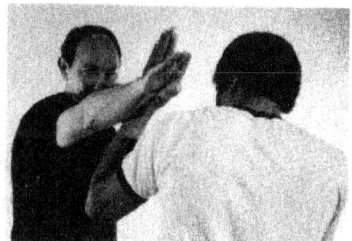

1. There is less chance of injuring your hand.
2. If your opponent blocks your attack, there is more chance of "sticking" to his arm since you're not meeting bone on bone. Sticking to your opponent's arm is one of the keys to controlling it.

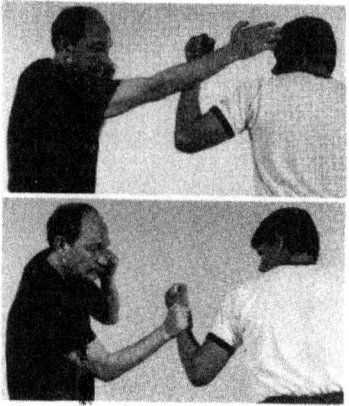

Palm hook

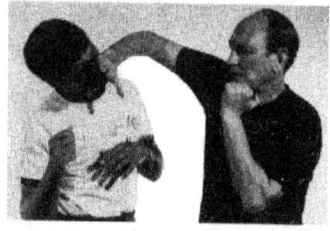

Strike your opponent's nose with the heel of your palm

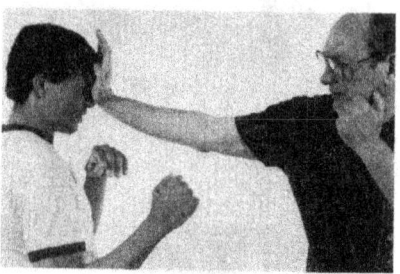

Snap down palm

Hsing-i smash

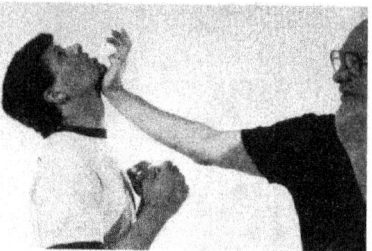

Tiger claw

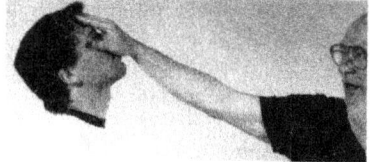

Willow leaf palm

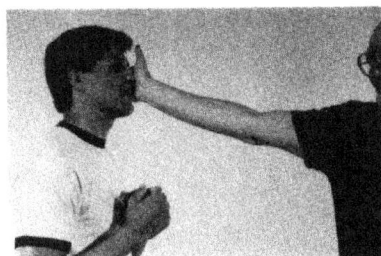

Side palm

Palm smash;

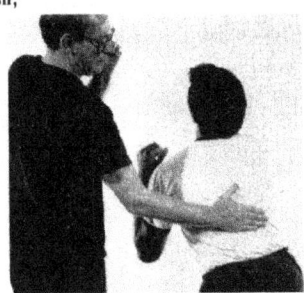

to spine

This downward smash can also be delivered to the kidney or to the base of the skull.

(E) FOREARM (Front/Rear)

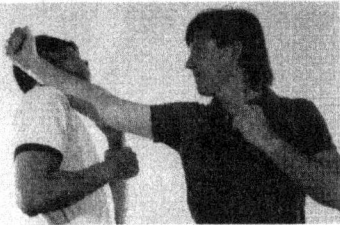

Back of

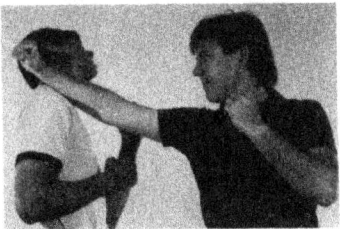

Side of

Inside of

(F) ELBOW (Front/Rear)

Vertical upward

Vertical downward

Diagonal upward

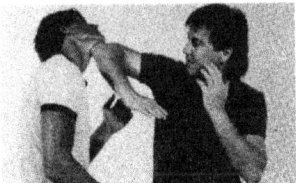

Backward diagonal upward

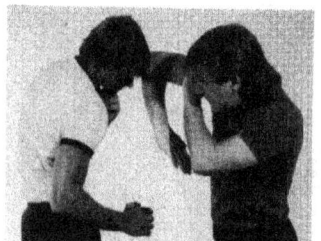
Diagonal downward

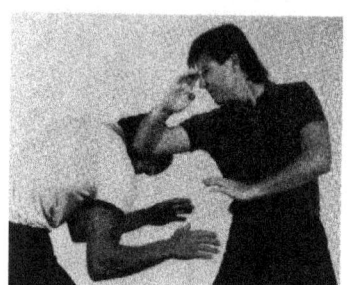
Backward diagonal downward

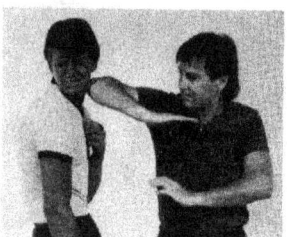
Horizontal

Backward horizontal

(G) SHOULDER BUTTING (Front/Rear)

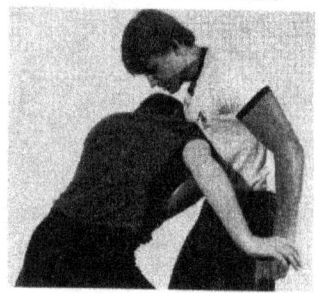

(H) FOOT STOMPING (Front/Rear)

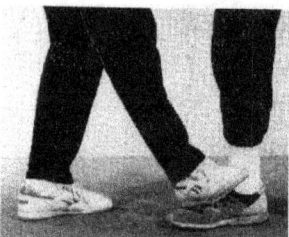
Hip opening

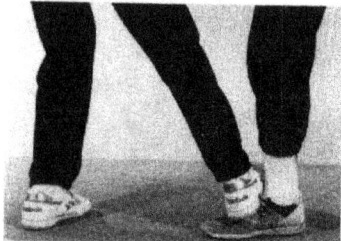
Hip closing

Backward

(I) HEADBUTTING

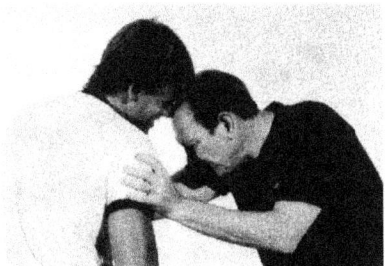
Front

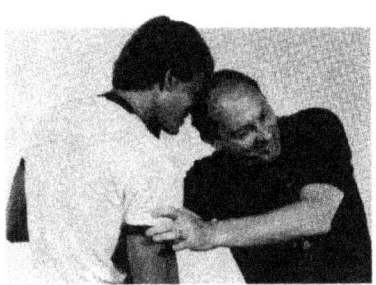
Side

Back

(J) SPINNING BLOWS Also called pivot blows

Spinning backfist

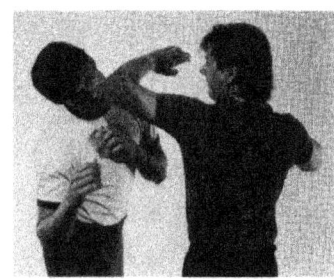
Spinning elbow

(K) PRESSURE POINTS AND "DIRTY FIGHTING"

When your life or the life of your loved one is at stake there is no such thing as "dirty fighting." When you find yourself in such a life or death situation, survival is the only important thing. Biting, pinching, and gouging are useful tools which can be used for the following reasons:

1. To escape from a hold.
2. To restrain your opponent.
3. To force your opponent to submit.
4. As a transition to another technique.

a. Biting

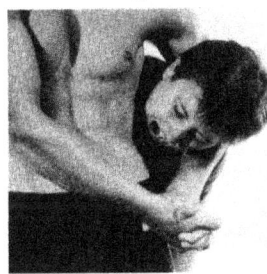 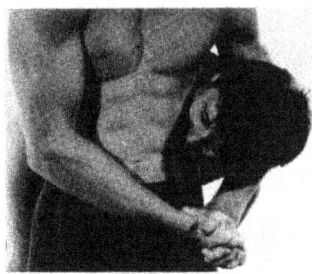

b. Squeezing
1. The groin (not shown)

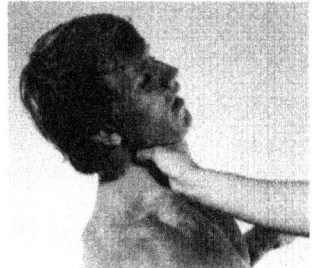

2. The throat

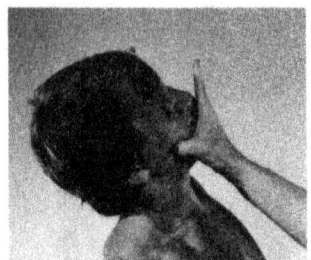

3. The nerves on the side of the jaw

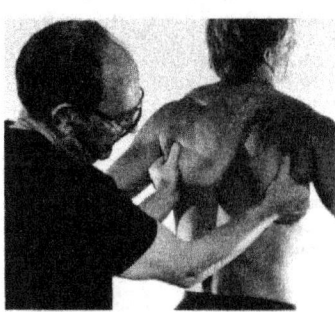

4. Two hands at the armpit

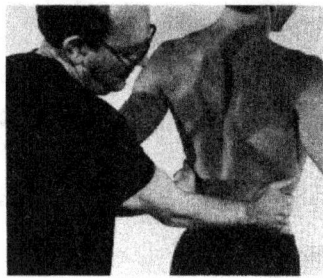

5. Two hands at the side

   c. Twist and Pull (the following list is self-explanatory and needs no illustrations)
    1. The ear
    2. The bottom lip
    3. The cheek
    4. The eyelid

d. Pinch
   Good places to pinch are the inner thigh and the inner arm between the bicep and the tricep.

e. Gouging and Tearing

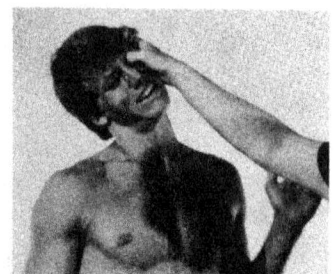

1. The eye

2. The mouth

f. Squeezing or Pressing on Pressure Points
   Experiment until you can find the proper spot immediately and without looking. Make sure you use the tips of your fingers.

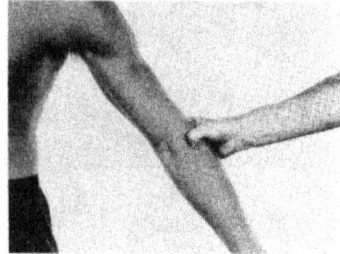

1. The forearm

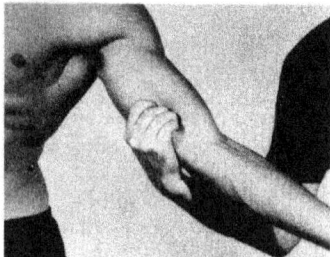

2. The upper arm

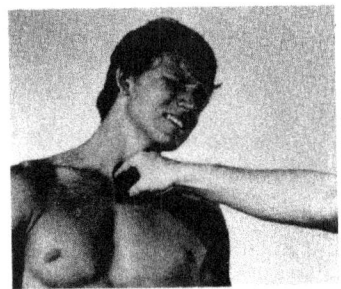
The hollow of the throat

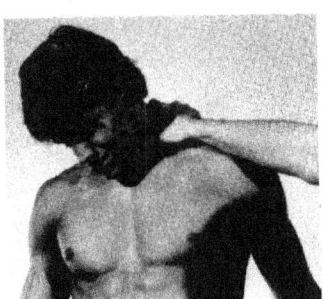
The side of the neck

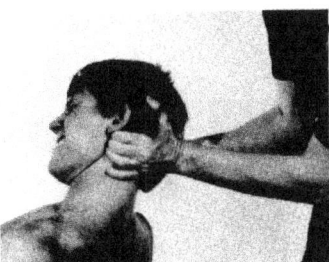
Behind the ear

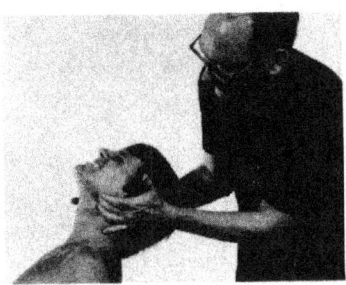
Under the jaw

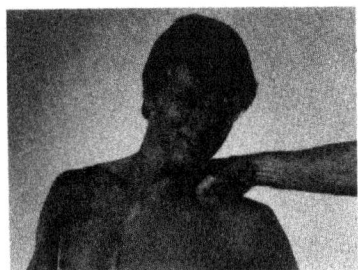
Behind the collar bone

(G) HAIR PULLING
To achieve the maximum amount of pain, hair should be pulled up rather than down.

These are the various striking weapons and striking surfaces used in Jun Fan training. For a more detailed description of specific tools such as jab, cross, hook, etc., refer to "Jeet Kune Do Kickboxing." The main point is that at times you can alter the striking surface you use in your attack. For instance, you may use a rear cross attack but land with a palm smash instead of a fist.

Various weapons are best used solely for long-range fighting, others are better for in-fighting. Certain tools may be used at long, intermediate, and close range. Two examples are:

A lead hook punch to the face.

A lead hook kick to the groin.

THE USE OF THE LEG OBSTRUCTION

The leg obstruction plays a vital role in Jun Fan training. It can be used effectively as an attack, a counterattack, or for defense. The leg obstruction differs from a low sidekick in that it is basically a stiff-legged lift,

whereas a low sidekick is a thrusting, piston-like action.

Some examples may be:
1. Using a leg obstruction to bridge the gap into punching.

3. Using a leg obstruction to defend against an opponent's attempted kick.

2. Using a leg obstruction to bridge into trapping.

WEAPON DEVELOPMENT

The primary objective of tool training is the cultivation and concentration of power, and the development of speed and explosiveness along with precision and accuracy against a moving target. It means the ability to be able to use a particular tool from any position and while moving.

In the beginning stage a student usually concentrates on developing his attacking motion while advancing, but again, you should train to be able to fire a weapon while moving in all directions. An example might be training the side kick:

1. From a natural stance.

3. Step and slide shuffle forward.

2. Ready stance using front leg.

4. Slide shuffle advance.

5. Kick and return to opposite stance.

6. Retreating with a step and slide shuffle first.

The same kick can also be done:
1. Stepping through and returning to original position.
2. Stepping through and stopping there in opposite stance.
3. Hopping (airborne).
4. Spinning with rear leg.
5. Sidestepping either direction.

Tool developing and maintenance is an ongoing and never-ending process. It takes years, but conscientious attention to the basics will ensure a higher measure of success in the more technical and tactical aspects of fighting.

HAND IMMOBILIZATION AND ENERGY DRILLS

The terms, hand immobilization attack or trapping hands, refer to an attacking action which momentarily immobilizes either one or both of the opponent's arms, allowing your final hit to score in an open line, or drawing a reaction which can be countered either with another trap or by shifting into another aspect such as punching, grappling, etc. Trapping allows you to maneuver your opponent's arms where you want them and forces the opponent to give you a reaction which will be to their own detriment.

One of the primary objectives in trapping is to gain an "attachment" (touching one or both of the opponent's arms with your own arms), much like two fencers when they engage their blades. This attachment may be gained either offensively (off your attack) or defensively (off of opponent's attack). By understanding what trapping actions can be used from where your arms are at in relation to your opponent's arms (both hands outside, one hand inside—one hand outside, etc.), as well as by feeling the type of energy the opponent reacts with (forward, upwards, etc.), you can tie up one or both arms of the opponent and gain a split second's advantage in which to score.

MAJOR POINTS FOR H.I.A.

1. Control the centerline by occupying the centerline.

2. Maintain a well-covered on-guard position while closing the distance to trap. Be in good balance and keep your own boundaries closed.

CORRECT: The attacker shoots a lead punch at opponent's midsection to draw an attachment. In this case it is the opponent's lead hand. Notice the attacker's rear hand is well up, offering protection against any counter punch. The attacker then traps the opponent's lead arm while simultaneously firing a backfist into the open line.

INCORRECT: In this instance the attacker lets his rear guard drop, allowing the opponent an opportunity to counterpunch with a rear cross.

3. Be alert and aware of opponent's attempt to stop hit or counterattack.

The attacker shoots a lead jab at the high line to attack. As the attacker traps with pak sao, the opponent fires a rear cross counter. The attacker simultaneously parries the punch with a tan sao and punches with the opposite hand.

4. Control your position to enable you to angle strike when opponent opens up or backs up.

In this example as the attacker traps the opponent's arm with a pak sao, the opponent retreats in an attempt to escape. The attacker immediately fires a rear hook kick into the opponent's thigh.

5. Use feints and false attacks sometimes to ensure safety and increase the chances of success.

In this example the attacker fires a false lead jab attack to draw the opponent's blocking reaction which the attacker then counters by simultaneously disengaging and trapping the opponent's blocking arm.

6. Cut into the opponent's tool to trap and stop any counter.

In this example, the attacker fires a false lead jab attack to draw the opponent's blocking reaction which he then counters by using a sliding leverage punch to cut across the opponent's arm and hit.

7. Maintain the trap for the necessary amount of time so as to prevent the opponent from freeing the arm which was to be immobilized and countering you.

In this example, the attacker releases the trap too soon, allowing his opponent to free his arm and counter with a jao sao palm hook.

8. Make sure you use constant forward pressure which is like water flowing through the smallest crack seeking an opening. Whether your opponent retreats or advances he feels an "alive" tension against his arms at all times affecting his motions and restricting him.

9. Against an opponent who keeps his midsection well covered and reacts to body blows by using his elbows to cover the attack, it is sometimes possible to draw an involuntary blocking response by hitting directly into either arm instead of the body.

   a. The attacker punches into the opponent's lead forearm to draw a reaction then simultaneously disengages and traps the arm while hitting with a backfist.

   b. This time the attacker punches into the opponent's rear forearm to draw the reaction, disengages and traps the opponent's arm and lands a backfist.

10. Fighting an opponent who refuses to engage or attack with his lead arm requires the use of feints and false attacks in order to draw a reaction which may then be trapped.

In this example, the attacker shoots a false lead jab to the opponent's face to draw the opponent's attachment. The attacker then immobilizes the parry arm and scores with his real attack in an open line.

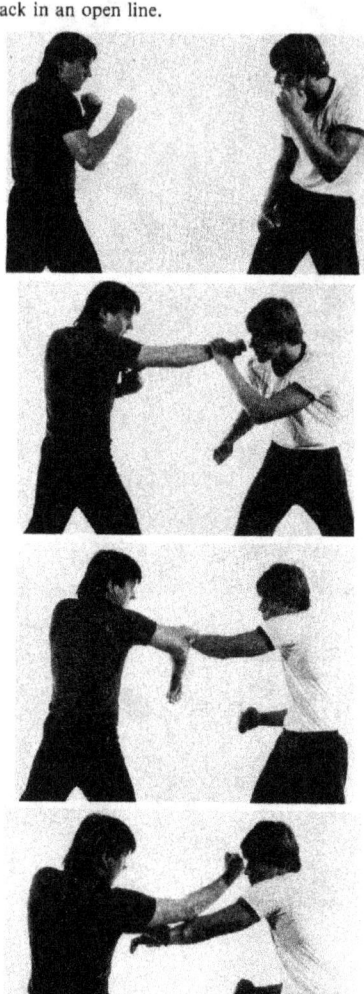

BASIC HAND IMMOBILIZATION ATTACKS (HIA)

The following photographs illustrate basic trapping actions in which you tie up either one or both of the opponent's arms with one hand while hitting with the other, depending upon which hand position your arms are in relation to the opponent's.

(I) PAK SAO (Slapping hand)

The pak sao is a palm slap to trap the arm. It can be done with the rear or lead hand. The important point is to control the opponent's arm by pushing into the centerline not by pulling down the hand, which can be countered easily.

(A) Pak Sao Pointers

1. Pak sao can be done at the wrist, forearm, or shoulder depending on opponent's range and position.

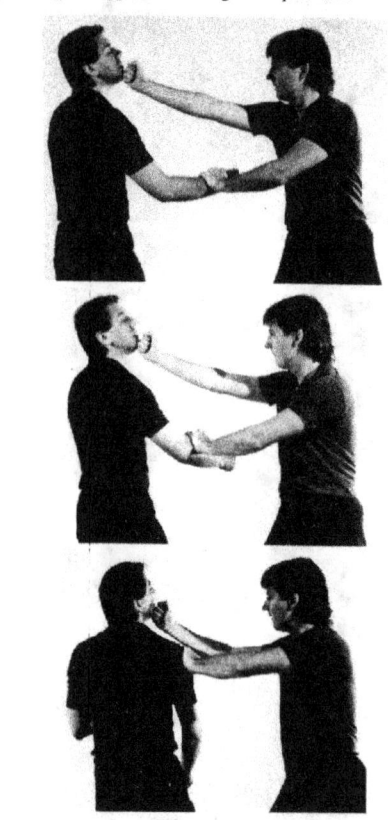

2. The pak sao can be practiced from the attached hand position, which is how you should first practice it to get the proper energy.

3. In combat the pak sao and punch can be used before, during and after an attack.
   a. As an attack (before).

b. As a defense as your opponent jabs you (during).

c. As a counterattack after your opponent has completed his attack (after).

4. Pak sao after a low kick. Kick then jab to get the attachment for the pak sao.

5. Pak sao can be done as a flow from one martial art to another. For example, from a Thai boxing stance and kick to pak and hit.

6. Pak sao can also be used as a defense against grappling.

(B) Examples of Different Lines of Attack Using Pak Sao:

1. Pak sao opponent's lead arm with rear hand and punch on outside of opponent's lead arm.

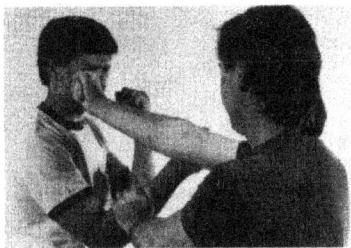

2. Pak sao opponent's lead arm with rear hand and punch on the inside of opponent's lead arm.

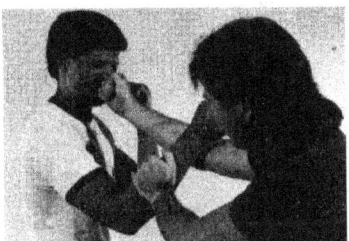

3. Pak sao opponent's lead arm with rear hand and punch on the outside of opponent's rear arm.

4. Pak sao opponent's rear arm (trapping front hand also) with your rear hand and punch on the inside of opponent's rear arm.

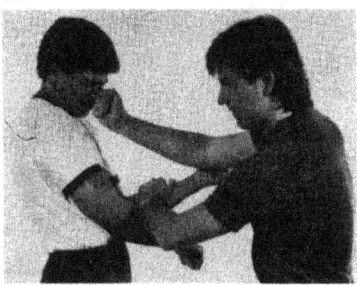

5. Pak sao opponent's rear arm (trapping front hand also) with rear hand and punch on the outside of opponent's rear arm.

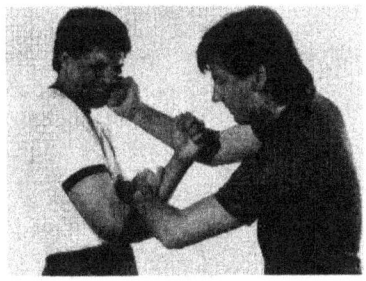

6. Pak sao opponent's lead arm on inside (trapping rear arm also) with lead hand and punch with rear hand.

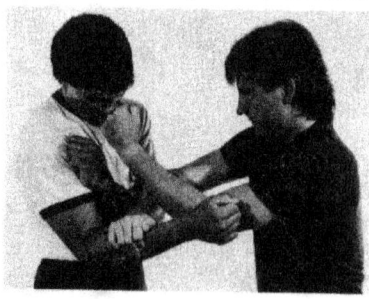

7. Pak sao opponent's lead arm on inside (trapping rear arm also) and punch with rear hand.

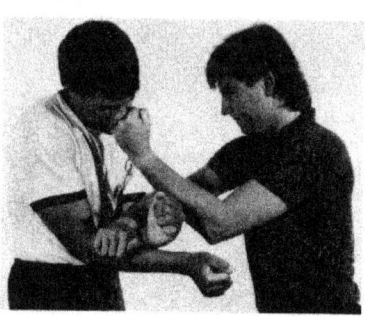

(II) LOP SAO (Grabbing Hand)

Lop sao can be defined as a grabbing and pulling motion against the arm.

(A) Examples of Lop Sao and Various Lines of Attack:

1. Lead hand lop sao on the outside of opponent's lead arm and rear hand punch on the outside of his arm.

2. Lead hand lop sao on the inside of opponent's rear arm and rear hand punch on the outside of opponent's lead arm.

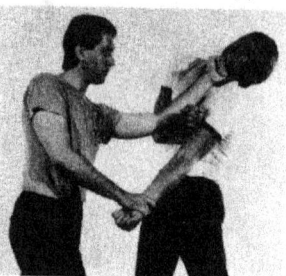

3. Lead hand lop sao on the inside of opponent's rear arm and rear hand punch on the inside of opponent's lead arm.

4. Rear hand lop sao on the inside of opponent's lead arm and lead hand punch on the inside of opponent's rear arm.

5. Rear hand lop sao inside of the opponent's lead arm and lead hand punch on outside of opponent's rear arm.

(III) JAO SAO (Running Hand)

Jao sao can be defined as a disengagement from the opponent's arms while moving from one line to another. Jao sao can be done from the outside line to the inside line, inside to outside, low to high and high to low.

(A) Examples of Jao Sao and Lines of Attack:

1. From a high outside reference point, lead hand jao sao to outside of opponent's rear arm.

2. From high outside reference point, lead hand jao sao to inside of opponent's rear arm.

3. From a high outside reference point, lead hand jao sao to the low inside line.

4. From a high outside reference point on opponent's rear arm, lead hand jao sao to the low inside line.

2. From double outside reference point rear hand jut sao opponent's arm and punch with lead hand.

3. From double outside reference point both hands jut sao and headbutt opponent's face.

(IV) JUT SAO (Short Snapping Hand)

Jut sao can be defined as a short sudden jerking motion against one or both of the opponent's arms. It can be used to (a) open a line; (b) distract; (c) draw a defensive reaction. It should be crisp and jolt the opponent.

(A) Jut Sao Examples:

1. From a double outside reference point, lead hand jut sao opponent's rear arm and punch with rear hand.

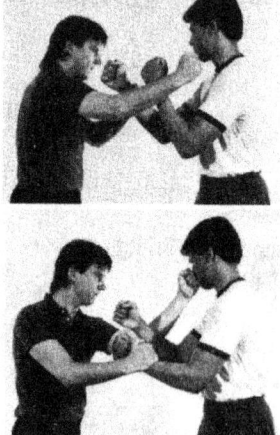

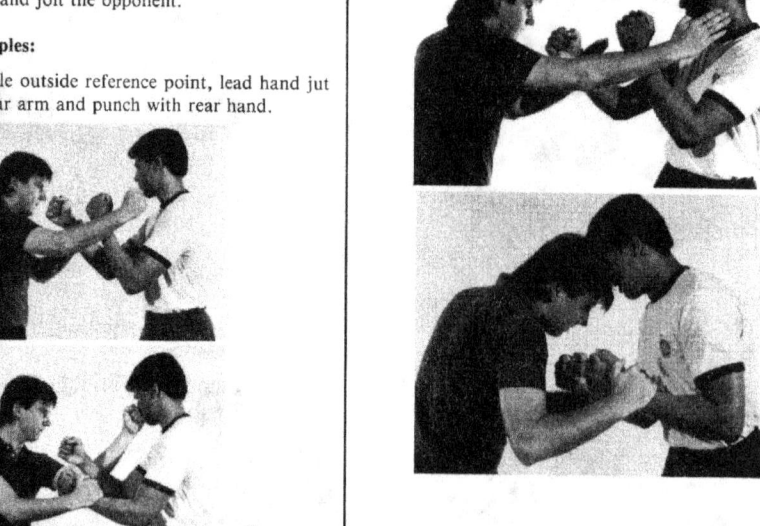

4. You can also jut sao on the inside high reference point as you punch with your rear hand on the high outside line of your opponent.

(V) HUEN SAO (Circling Hand)

Huen sao can be defined as a small disengagement either from the outside to the inside line or from the inside to the outside line of the opponent. This motion differs from jao sao in that huen sao maintains contact with the opponent's arm.

(A) Huen Sao Examples:

1. From a high rear outside reference point the attacker uses a lead hand huen sao to move around the opponent's rear arm to an inside position and punch.

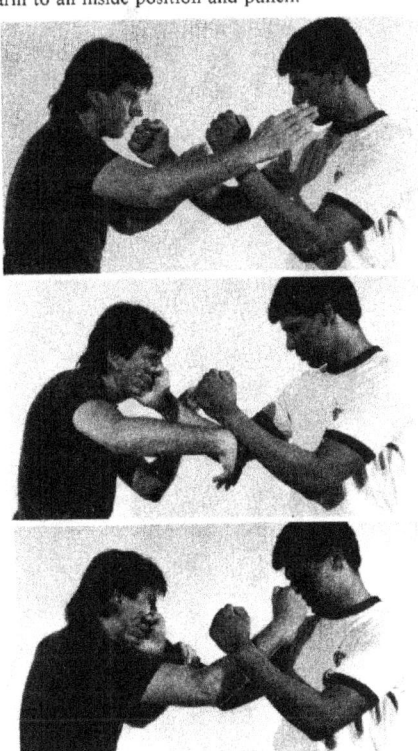

2. From a high outside reference point the attacker uses a rear hand huen sao to move around the opponent's lead hand to an inside position and punch.

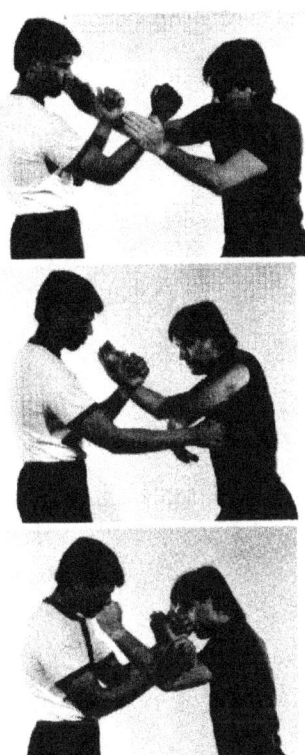

4 EXAMPLES OF HIA COMBINATIONS

1. Pak sao, sliding leverage hit, inside pak sao with punch.

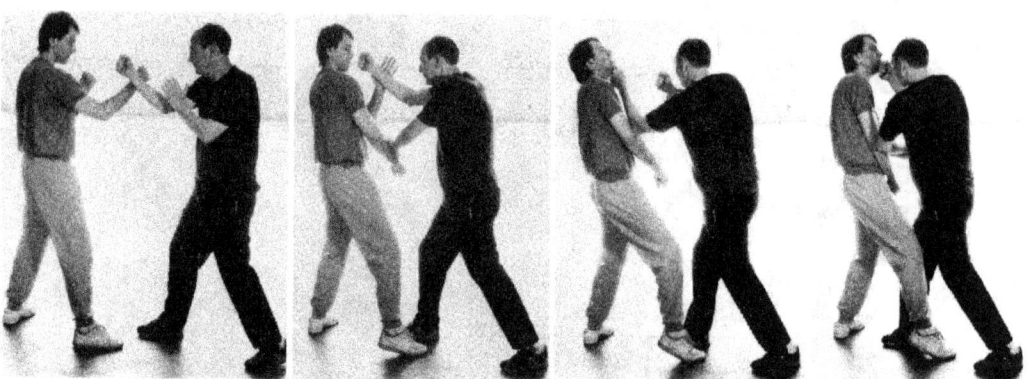

2. Lead hand lop sao with rear punch, rear hand huen sao, lead hand pak sao with rear hand sat sao.

3. Pak sao, scoop arm to open line and hammerfist to kidney.

4. Lead hand jao sao to outside rear line, lead jao sao to inside line and jut sao neck with rear punch.

FINAL NOTES ON HIA

(A) One must be able to shift from hand immobilization attack into other forms of attack and vice versa should the situation arise. You may, for example:

1. Shift from trapping to punching Western boxing style.

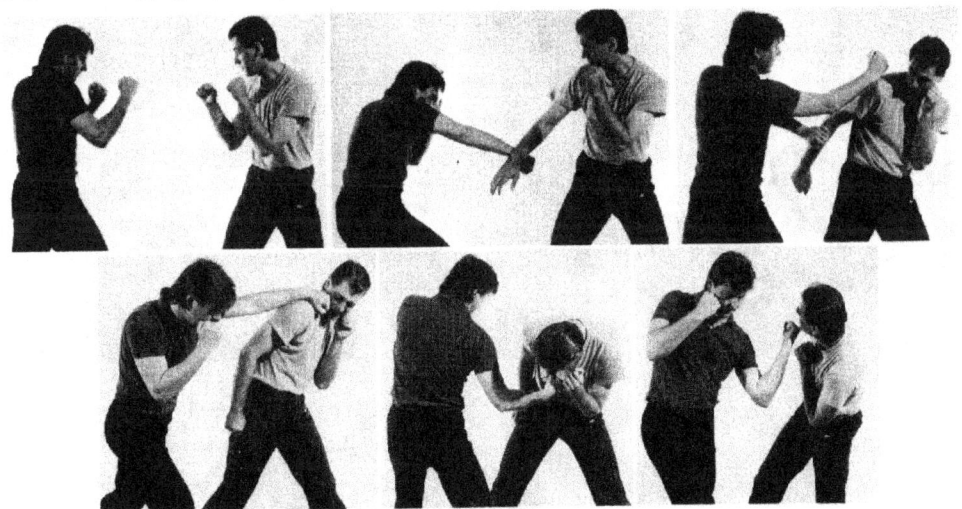

2. Shift from trapping to Muay Thai.

3. Trap and trip.

4. Trap and throw.

5. Shift from trapping to grappling.

6. Trap and choke.

7. Trap and takedown.

8. Trap and lock.

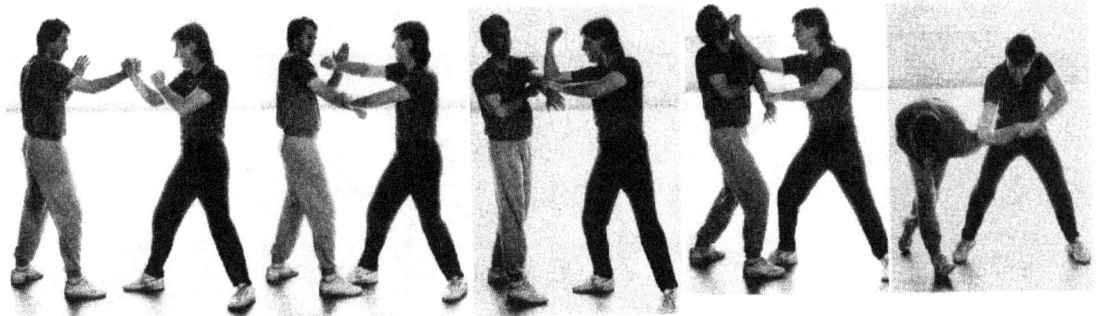

(B) One should also be able to flow into trapping from any other form of attack. An example may be:

1. Shift from boxing to trapping.

TRAINING AIDS IN HIA

1. Trapping is trained from the nucleus outwards. By nucleus we mean from trapping range with touch.

Then to bridging from kicking range, to punching range, to trapping range.

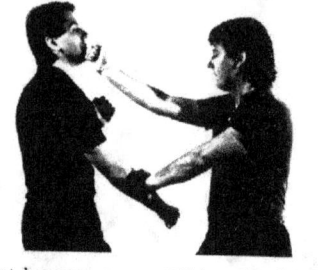

As a student becomes more proficient the distance is increased to punching range.

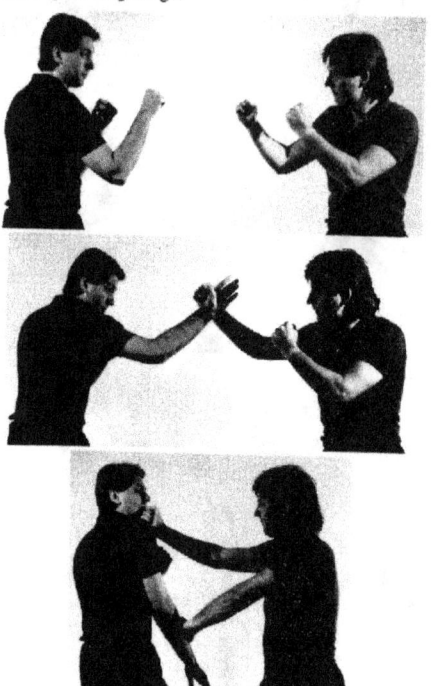

Then trapping should be combined with other fighting methods, i.e., boxing, wrestling, Muay Thai, etc. The reason for this progression is that most fights end up in close range very quickly.

2. Trapping should also be trained while sparring with boxing gloves.

3. Work on trapping with your eyes shut to increase sensitivity and awareness.

FOOT IMMOBILIZATION ATTACK (FIA)

Just as the opponent's arms may be immobilized to prevent them from being able to hit or parry, so can the opponent's legs be immobilized to prevent them from kicking or being used to escape. You can immobilize the opponent's foot by:

1. Stepping on it.

2. Locking the leg.

STOPPING

We have included stopping in this chapter because stopping is defined as the pinning of the opponent's hand or arm to prevent him from delivering a blow. It can be used:

1. As a preventative measure when attacking with one hand while pinning the other. In this case the attacker smothers the opponent's lead arm while firing his own lead hook to the face.

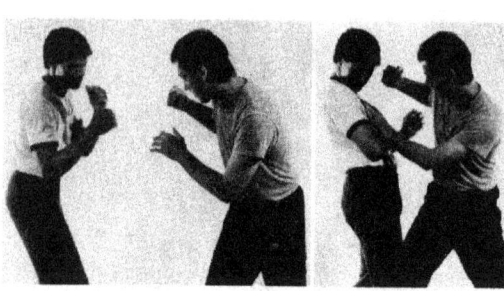

2. As a preventative measure when slipping or countering. Here the attacker slips inside the opponent's lead punch and smothers the opponent's rear hand while countering with his own rear punch.

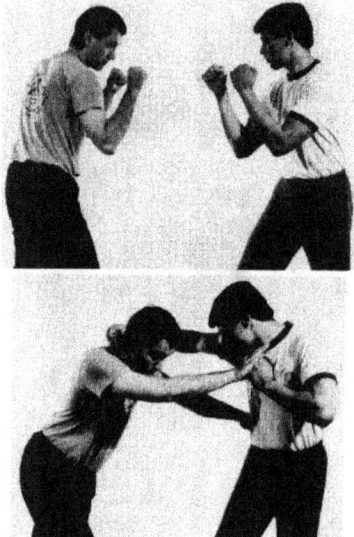

3. When an opponent actually intends to deliver a blow (requires knowledge of when opponent is going to hit and depends upon speed and skill for execution). The attacker smothers the opponent's telegraphic pull back before punching, and immediately counters with his own rear punch.

ENERGY/SENSITIVITY TRAINING

*When he comes, take him there
When he goes, follow
When there is emptiness, HIT!*

An integral and essential ingredient in understanding hand immobilization attack is appreciation and understanding of "energy." By energy we mean the force given against any attacking motion by the opponent. This understanding enables you to "feel" what the opponent is attempting to do, what direction his body force is going, using the sense of touch. With sensitivity and tactile awareness you don't even need to see where your hands are in relation to the opponent because you feel it. Using this awareness you can take your opponent's energy and dissolve it, redirect it, or bounce it away. Let's look at some of the different energies an opponent can give you with their lead or rear hand:

Straight forward

LEAD HAND:

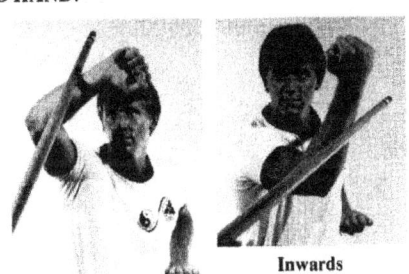

Inwards

Upwards

Outwards

Downwards

REAR HAND:

Stopping at centerline   Crossing centerline

From centerline outwards   Catching

51

Grabbing inwards   **Grabbing outwards**

The following training drills were developed to increase your awareness of energy, and to improve your sensitivity of touch and feel. They will also help you to learn economy of motion and develop your own constant flowing energy. The exercises themselves are *NOT* designed to teach you how to fight. If you cannot take the sensitivity you develop while practicing the exercises and use it in an alive, combative situation, then it is useless and "dead."

(I) ENERGY DRILLS

(A) Basic Drill to Feel Energy: The following is a simple and basic drill to feel an opponent's energy. It should first be done with the eyes open. Then closed.

1. From the attached hand position your training partner shoves his hand straight forward. You then dissolve it with a tan sao as you punch his face. (All examples are shown with your hit connecting. Make sure you control your punches in practice.)

2. From the beginning position your partner pushes your arm up. You then outside parry and punch low.

3. Your partner shoves your arm to the right. Letting your elbow hinge relax (see swinging gate drill) you inside lop with your rear hand and hit with a hammerfist.

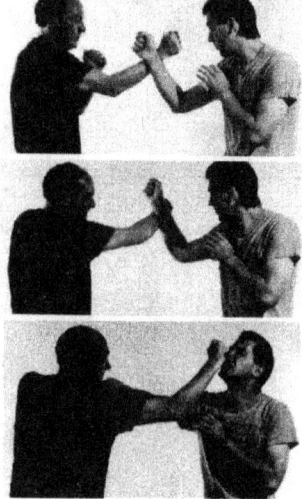

4. When your partner hits low, punch forward as you block with your rear hand.

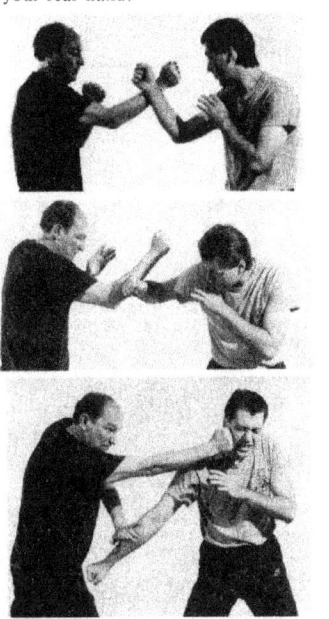

When you can do each one of the above without looking, your partner should mix the 4 up so you don't know which one he is going to do. Once you have mastered this drill move on to the next one.

(B) Harmonious Spring Drill

This exercise has its origins in the Preying Mantis gung fu system, and has been modified and included in the Jun Fan curriculum because it aids in developing: (a) bridging energy, and (b) dissolving energy.

BEGINNING HARMONIOUS SPRING DRILL

This drill starts with your training partner's arms on the outside of your arms. He then does a double jut sao and tries to touch your forehead. You control his energy by springing upwards while controlling the centerline and touching him on his forehead.

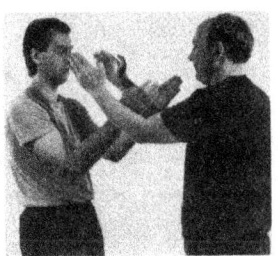

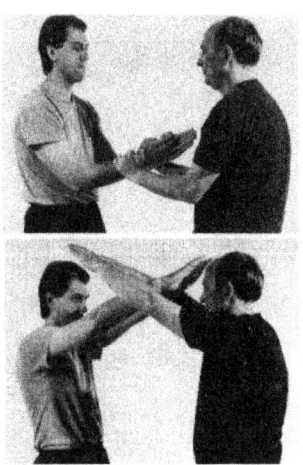

ONE HAND HARMONIOUS SPRING DRILL

In the ready position the trainer has the inside of his forearm touching the outside of the student. The trainer pulls the student's arm downward, using jut sao to open the line. The student neither resists the pull nor loosely goes with it. Rather he imagines a spring being stretched between his bicep and forearm.

BRIDGING

1. As the trainer slides his arm forward to punch, the student deflects the punch by bridging forward with a biu jee (finger jab).

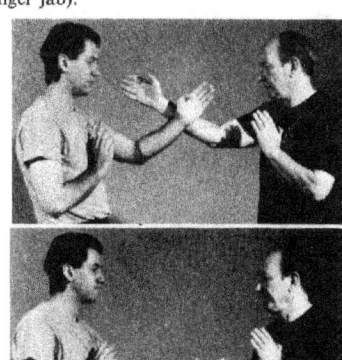

53

2. This time the student uses a tan sao bridge.

3. This time the student uses a boang sao (but without waist twist to develop proper arm position).

DISSOLVING

Dissolving the attacker's energy means that you redirect the force and bounce it or slide it away so that it does not hit you.

1. The student combines waist pivot with the boang sao to redirect the force.

2. The student pivots the opposite direction and dissolves the force using a tan sao.

The harmonious spring drill can be practiced two ways:
1. Harmonious, to develop sensitivity and proper position as in the above drills.
2. Combative, to develop timing and reactions as in the following drill.

TWO MAN SLIDING LEVERAGE, JUT SAO, HARMONIOUS SPRING DRILL

The following drill allows you to work on three attributes at the same time:
1. Using sliding leverage against a punch.
2. Practicing jut sao and hit.
3. And practicing harmonious spring energy.

Start the drill by facing each other. You have your right hand forward while your partner has his left hand forward. When your partner punches with his left hand, cross parry with your left as you hit with your right. You should be able to block and hit with your right arm only as you move his attacking arm aside with sliding leverage. The cross parry is merely a safety factor. Your partner then juts and hits with his left hand. You then dissolve it with a harmonious spring as you hit with a finger jab to his eyes.

Below is an example of sliding leverage without the cross parry.

Then your partner punches with his right arm. Your right arm comes back into a cross parry as your left does a sliding leverage and you repeat using your left arm.

(B) SWING GATE DRILL
(Elbow Hinge/Ball and Socket Drill)

Stand facing each other in a natural stance. As the attacker uses an inward forearm block against the outside of his partner's arm, his partner uses his elbow as a hinge and while maintaining a covered centerline with his upper arm and rear hand, allows the blocking energy to travel through while simultaneously trapping the arm and firing a backfist. Note that the trap is over the arm as the attacker's arm is above.

Here the attacker uses a palm slap to block, so the partner traps from under his own arm as that is where the handle is.

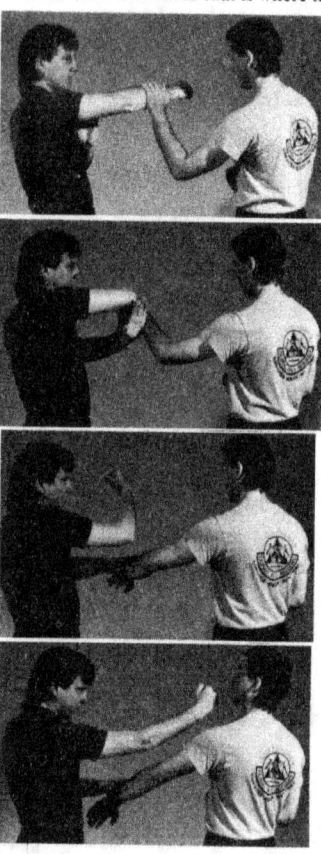

Here the attacker uses an inward forearm block against the inside of his partner's arm. The partner uses the ball and socket joint of his arm, allowing the blocking energy to travel through while trapping the arm and firing a backfist. *Note:* In this motion it doesn't matter whether the attacker uses his forearm or his palm to block.

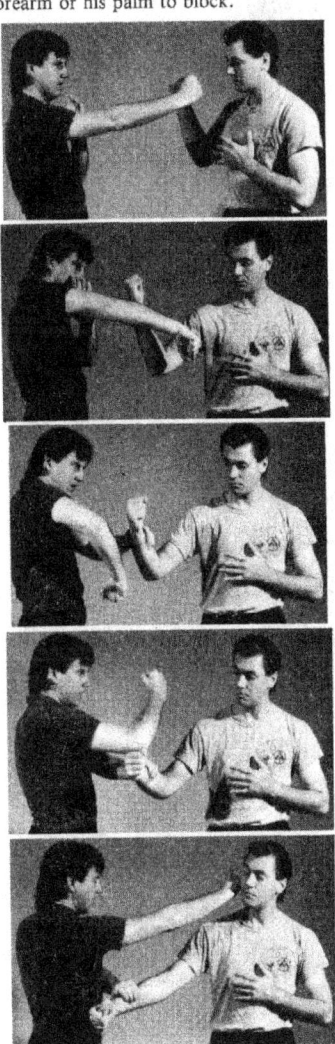

The above examples were done with touch. That is, you allow the blocker to make contact with your arm thus propelling it. Another method is to use sensitivity. That is, to not allow the block to make contact. Below are two examples:

1.

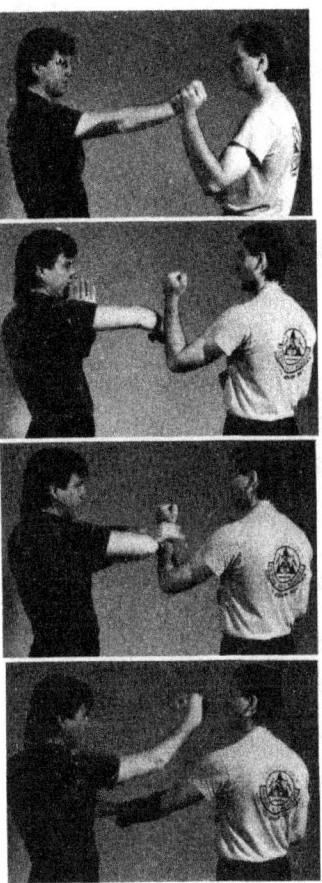

2.

Once you can do all of the above with both arms follow this progression.
1. The blocker hits either the inside or outside of your arm while not letting you know which one he is going to do.
2. Do the same but you use sensitivity instead of touch.
3. Do with either sensitivity or touch.
4. Do with your eyes closed.

TACTICAL APPLICATIONS
Here we see the same drills used in a combative situation.

1. The attacker shoots a lead straight punch, as the defender attempts a forearm block the attacker simultaneously dissolves the energy and traps the arm, firing a backfist.

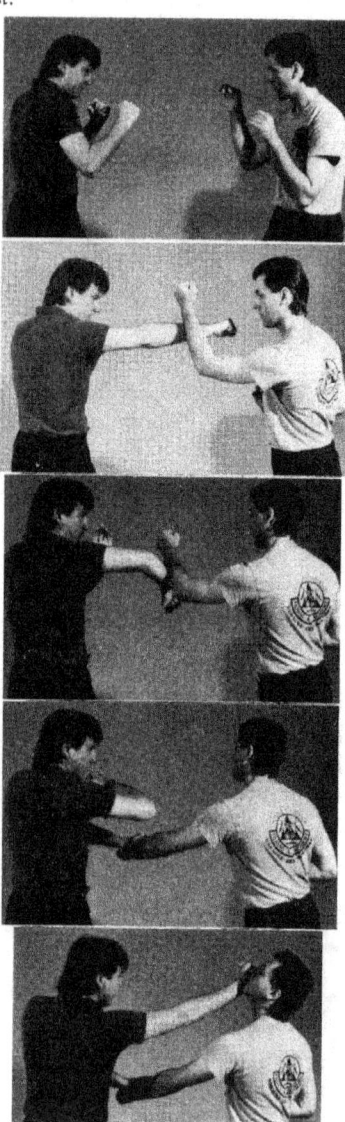

2. The attacker shoots a lead straight punch and as the opponent attempts a lead forearm block inwards, the attacker uses his ball and socket joint to go with the force and traps and hits.

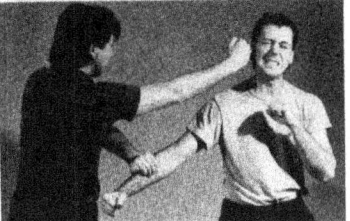

TRAINING AID (FOR #1 & 2)
Do the above while having the defender block with either his front or rear arm while you "flow" with the energy.
Do with touch.
Do with sensitivity.
Do with either touch or sensitivity.
It is important that you do all of the above drills slowly until you can do them at full speed as the defender blocks with full power.

(C) BOANG SAO—LOP SAO DRILL
This drill is from Wing Chun and is designed so that you and your partner can work on the following:
1. Practicing the lop sao.
2. Working with the boang sao as defense.
3. Practicing various attacks and switches.
4. Defending against various attacks.

The basic drill can be practiced with either the backfist

or the vertical punch.

1. Basic Boang Sao—Lop Sao Roll with the Backfist.

Stand facing each other. The man on the left has his left arm in a boang sao position. The man on the right grabs his partner's left wrist while resting his right forearm and his partner's boang sao. The man on the left then lops his partner's arm and backfists. It is important that when your arm is pulled you release your grab or the bottom wrist so you can flow within the confines of the drill. The man on the right then blocks the backfist with his boang sao, lops, and backfists, and so on.

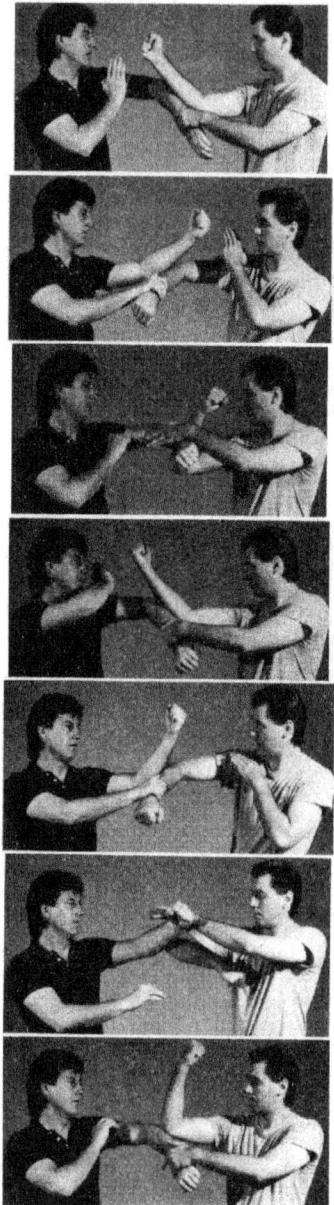

2. The Roll with a Vertical Punch.

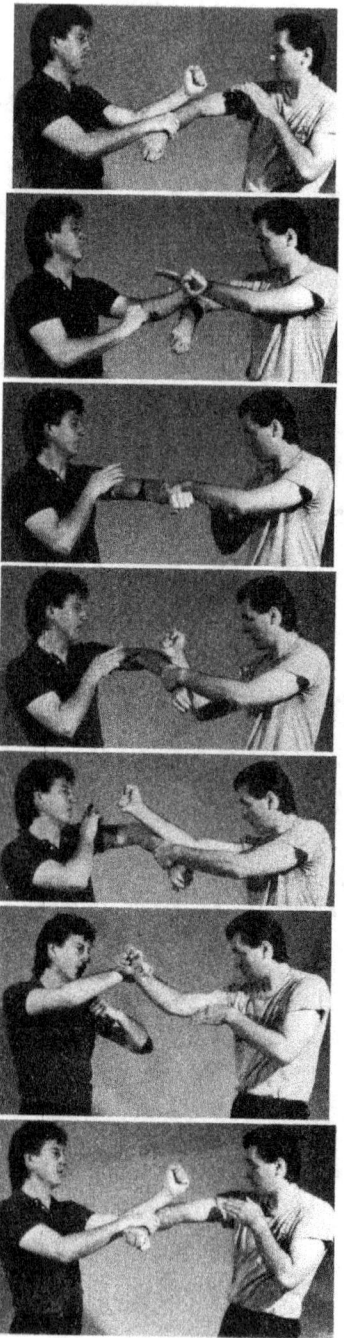

3. The High Lop Sao Switch. (Switch means to go from one lead to the other. For example, from left lead against right lead to right lead against left lead.)

As your partner blocks your backfist or vertical punch, you switch leads by loping with the hand that has hit. Then hit with the opposite hand which your partner dissolves with a boang sao. You have now switched leads and can flow on the opposite side.

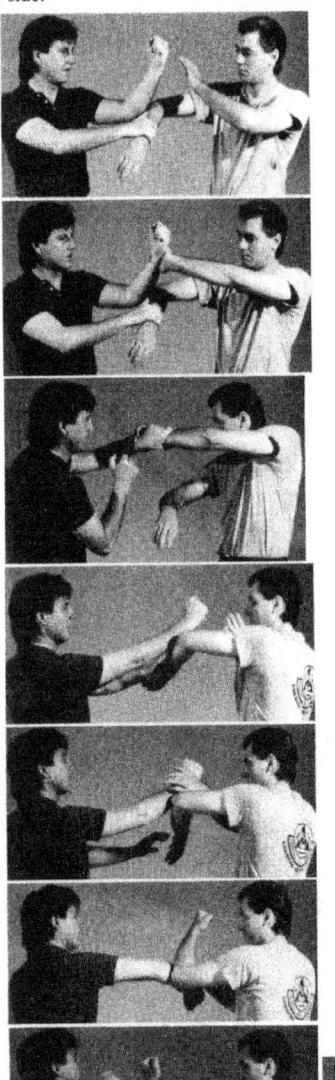

4. The High Tan Sao Switch.

As your partner grabs your punching arm and before he can hit you, tan sao and punch, thus switching sides.

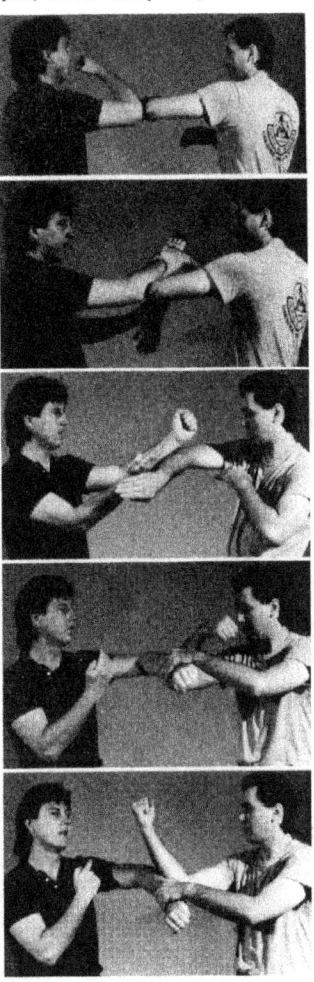

5. The Low Hand Lop Sao Switch.

After dissolving his punch with your boang sao, turn your boang sao over and lop with the same arm, as you punch with the opposite arm.

6. The Chop to the Side, Goang Sao Switch.

Instead of punching you chop to your partner's side which he blocks with a goang sao and punches. You then dissolve the punch by angling to the outside and punch using sliding leverage. Your partner then lops and punches to continue the flow.

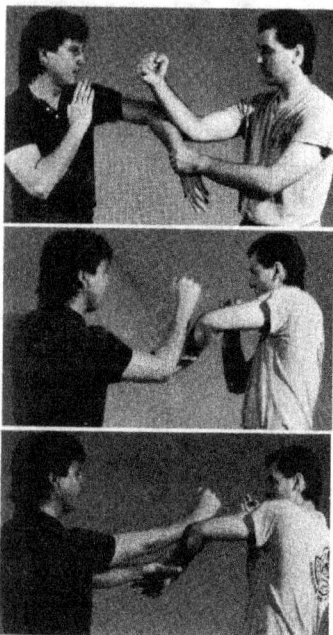

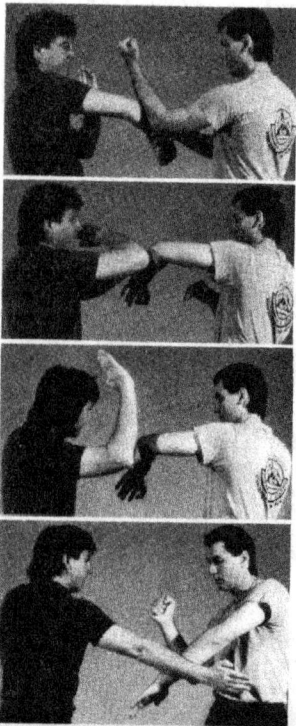

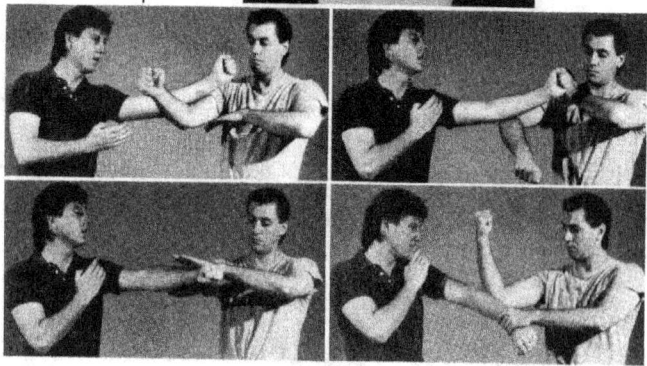

7. The Pak Sao Switch.

Fake as if you were going to backfist, but instead pak sao and punch which your partner then dissolves by angling to the outside and cutting into the tool with sliding leverage.

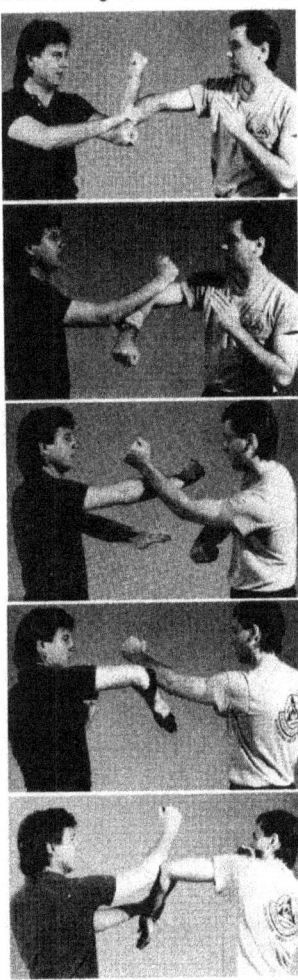

These are just a few of the many techniques that can be practiced. You could write a whole book just on this one drill alone. See if you can create your own techniques using this drill.

(D) CHI SAO

Chi sao (the art of the sticking hand) is a Wing Chun drill that is important for many reasons:

1. It helps the student to find the proper arm positions for Wing Chun techniques.
2. It helps to sharpen technical skill as all of the traps and hits of Wing Chun can be practiced.
3. It helps to sharpen the sense of touch.
4. It is a good way to practice using Wing Chun principles such as: (1) Thrust forward when the hand is freed. (2) Stay with what comes.
5. It can also help strengthen the shoulders.
6. It can help hone both your offensive and defensive reactions.
7. It can help you keep a constant energy flow between you and your partner.

It is very dificult to learn Chi Sao from a book as you need to feel the proper energy. If available we would recommend a good Wing Chun teacher.

1. Dan Chi (Single Hand)

a. Left is in a fook sao position. Right is in tan sao position.

b. Right moves his tan out to open up left's centerline. Then tries to slap his chest with a palm hit.

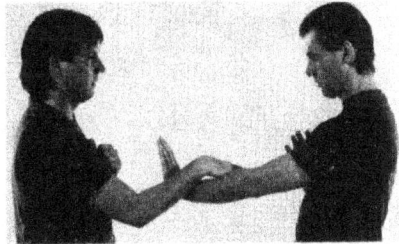

c. Left dissolves the attack by cutting into the tool with a vertical punch.

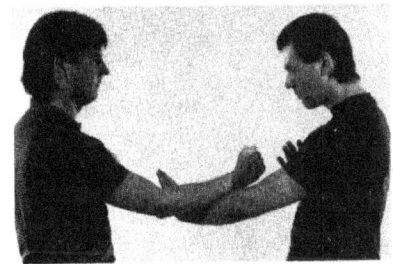

d. Right counters this with a boang sao.

e. Right's boang sao then turns into a tan sao and they return to their original positions.

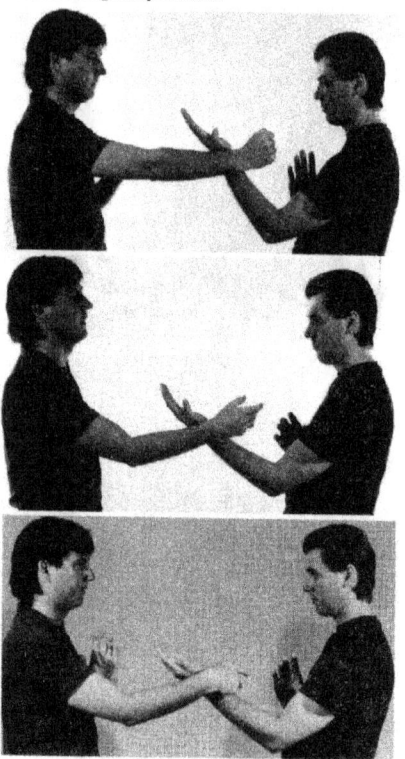

f. Another way to block the palm attack is with a cutting palm block.

After completing this block the man on the left shoots a vertical punch which the man on the right dissolves with a boang sao block.

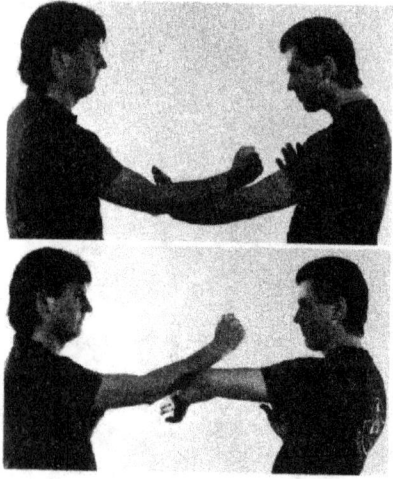

g. To Switch Sides: When the man on the left blocks right's palm strike, the man on the right, using swinging gate principle, rolls to a backfist. Left then blocks with a tan sao. Left is now in tan while right is in fook.

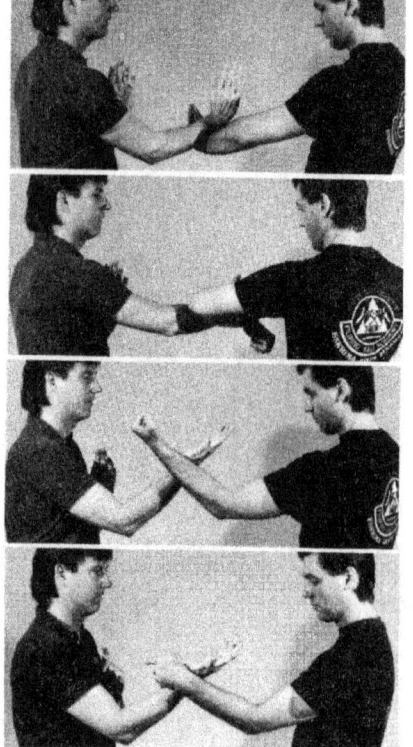

Here we see the switch performed by the man on the left after right's punch.

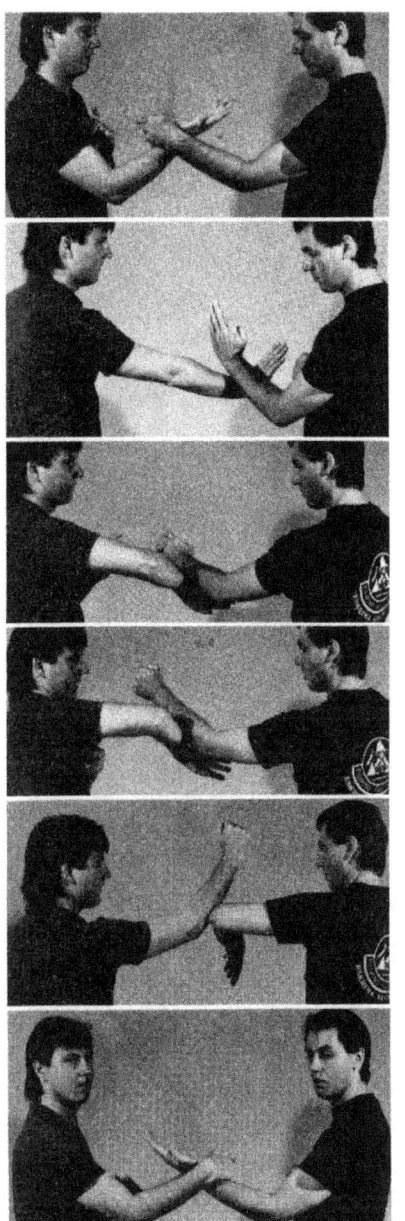

You should practice dan chi from the following hand positions and once you can flow with this exercise you should move on to 2 hand chi sao:

YOU	YOUR PARTNER
1. Right hand in fook	Left hand in tan
2. Right hand in tan	Left hand in fook
3. Left hand in fook	Right hand in tan
4. Left hand in tan	Right hand in fook

CHI SAO

Chi sao can be performed from the following stances:
1. Natural stance.
2. Both in right lead.
3. Both in left lead.
4. While moving.
5. While standing on one leg for balance.

(A) Chi sao can be performed with the following hand positions:

1. Right lead—The man on the left has his right arm in boang sao and his left arm in fook sao. The man on the right has his left arm in fook sao and his right is in boang sao.

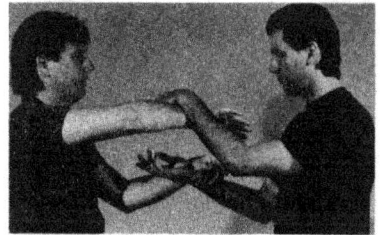

They then roll with a slight forward pressure until their positions are reversed.

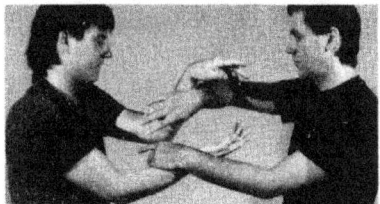

2. Left lead. Left arm shifts from tan to boang, right arm in fook sao.

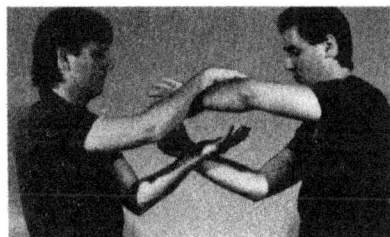

3. One man with both hands on the outside. The other man with both hands on the inside.

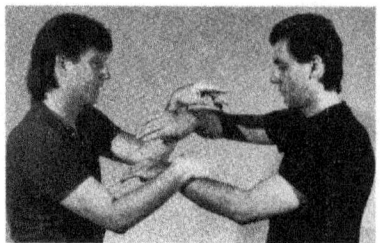

a. To roll from this position, the man on the left stays in fook sao while the man on the right goes from boang sao to tan sao.

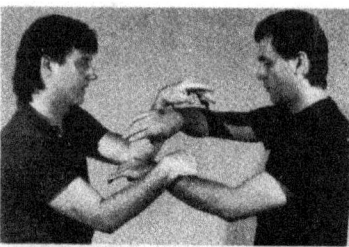

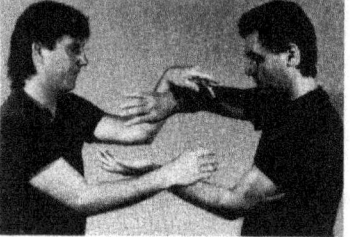

b. To switch from one lead to another, use huen sao. Below is a complete roll with switches.

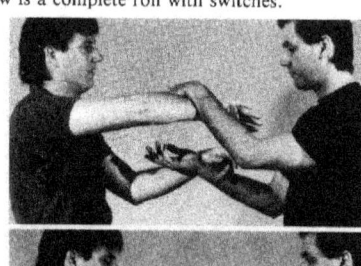

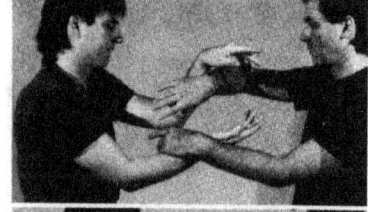

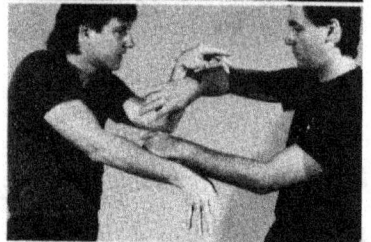

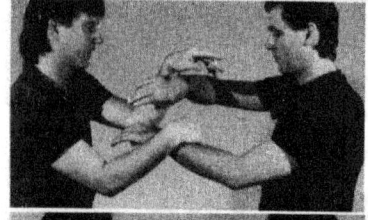

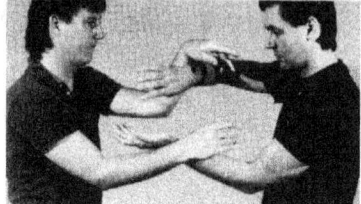

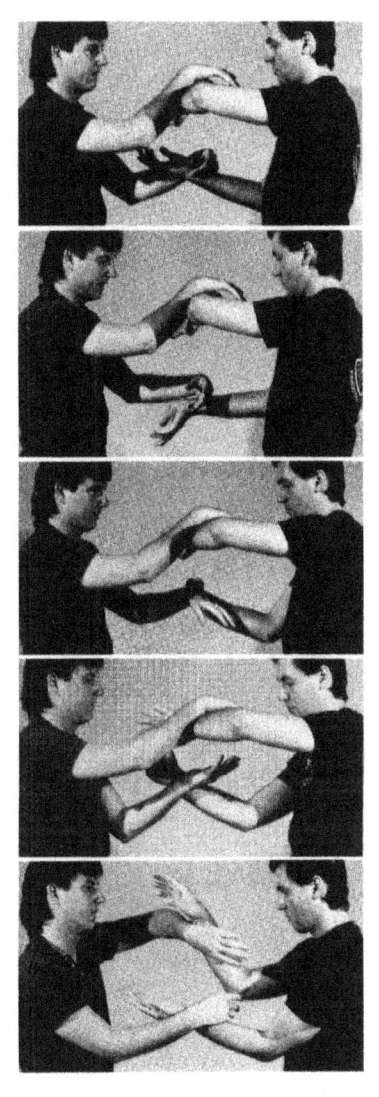
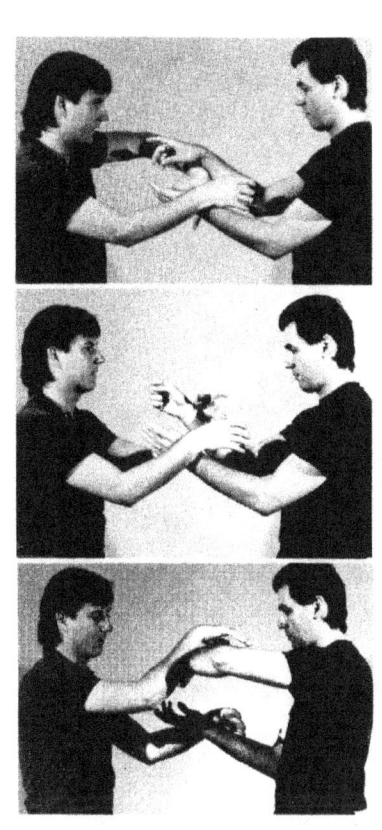

CHI SAO TRAINING EXERCISES

1. Take the Hand Away Drill:

This drill is designed to practice the Wing Chun principle of "thrusting forward when the hand is freed." In this drill the man on the left is acting as the trainer. As they roll he will *quickly* drop one of his arms. As soon as the man on the right feels this, he will immediately thrust forward with a controlled punch to the chest.

2. Push-Pull Chi Sao:

This drill is a good one for balance and for feeling your partner's energy. Using your forearms you and your partner attempt to push and pull each other off balance. To keep the "flow" of the exercise, once you have pushed your partner off balance, pull him back and vice versa.

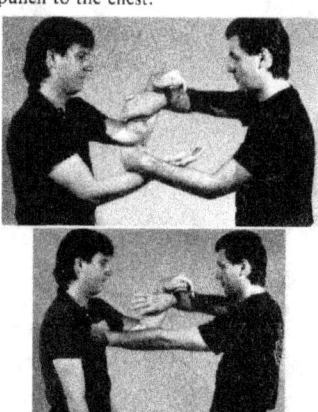
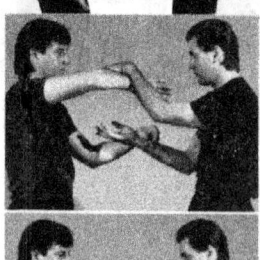

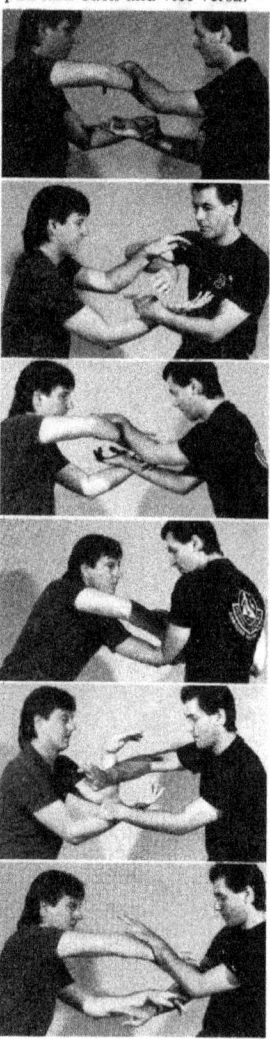

SOME HITTING AND TRAPPING TECHNIQUES

1. Right palm hit to chest.

    As your partner rolls up to fook, hit him in the chest with your right palm.

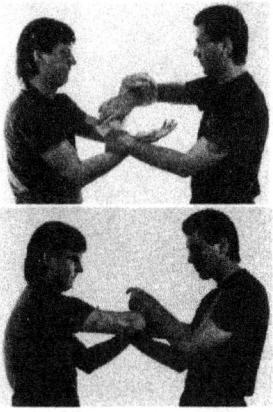

2. Right palm up finger jab to throat.

    As you roll down to tan, shoot a right hand palm up finger strike to the throat.

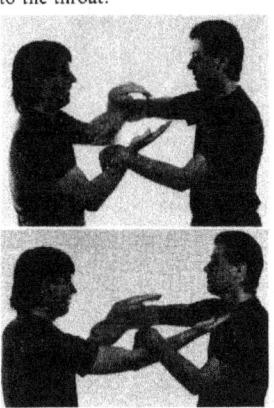

3. Left finger jab to eye.

    As your partner rolls up to boang, sneak your left hand over the top and hit the eye.

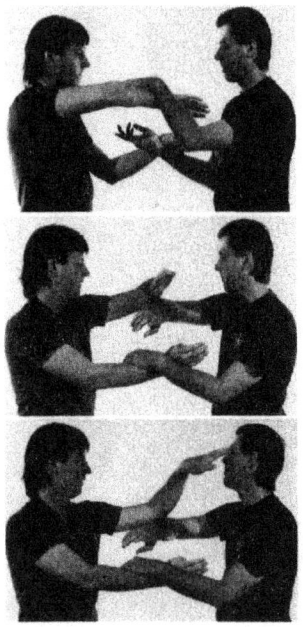

4. Inside Pak Sao.

    As your partner's left arm starts to drop, inside pak with your left hand, trapping his other arm at the same time, as you hit with your right.

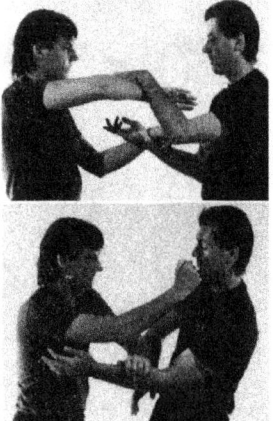

5. Low punch.
   As your partner's hand rolls to tan, hit him with a left low punch.

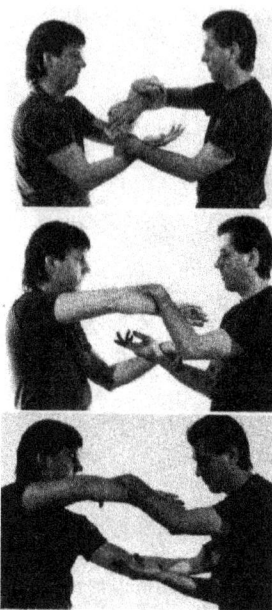

6. Lop Sao under the Bridge.
   As you roll up to boang sao, lop under your right arm and backfist.

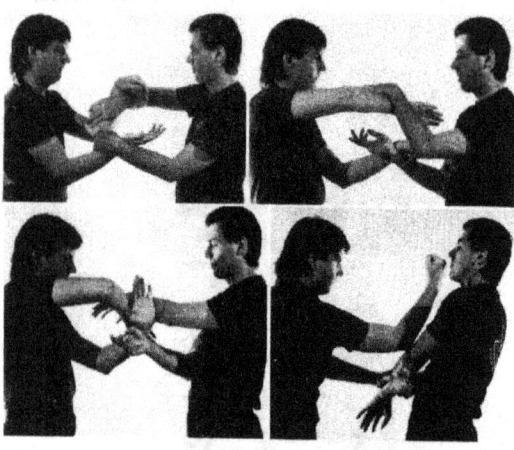

7. Lop Sao in Front of the Bridge.
   You can also lop in front of your right hand.

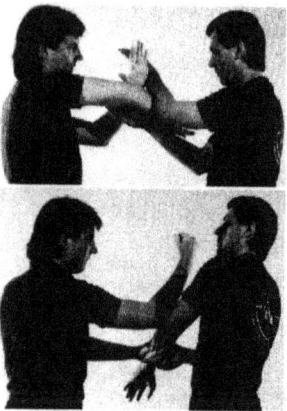

8. Low Grab and Pin with Punch.
   As your left fook starts to roll down, grab his right wrist with your right hand and punch as you pin his left arm with your right elbow.

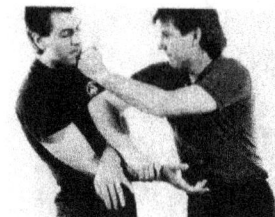

9. High Grab with Low Punch.
   As your partner's right arm is going up, grab it with your right hand and punch low. Notice how your right forearm controls his left arm.

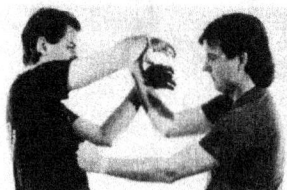

10. Inside Lop Sao to Pak Sao.
    As your partner is rolling up to boang sao, inside lop with your right hand as you hit with a left side palm strike to the face. Then left pak and hit a right side palm strike to the face.

11. Fake to Small Disengagement to Hit.

Fake is if you were going to hit with your right hand on the inside line. Then quickly disengage and hit to the outside line.

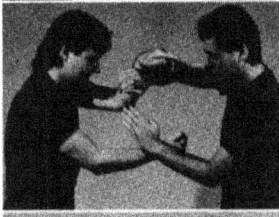

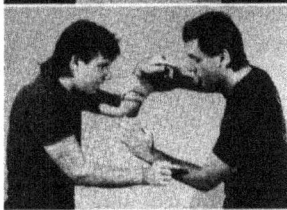

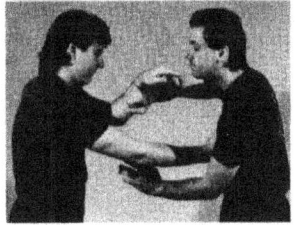

After working on these techniques, you should feel free to add other traps and hits. The next stage should include more combination traps and hits. Then counters to all of the above should be developed. Then counters to the counters. Then finally chi sao sparring.

While many of the energy drills in this chapter are complex and would need a whole series of books to cover fully, they are not the only energy drills a Jun Fan student works on. Other important energy drills are as follows:
 1. Wing Chun sticky legs drill.
 2. Pentjak Silat sticky foot drills.
 3. Hsing-i flow drill.
 4. Tai Chi pushing hands drill.
 5. Kali pushing hands drill.
 6. Kali Hu Bud Lu Bud drills.
 7. Kali roll drill.

We recommend that you seek out teachers who can teach you these drills.

AS FAR AS OTHER STYLES OR
SCHOOLS ARE CONCERNED
.... TAKE NO THOUGHT OF WHO IS
RIGHT OR WRONG   OR WHO IS
BETTER THAN. BE NOT FOR OR
AGAINST.
    FOR IN THE LANDSCAPE OF SPRING
THERE IS NEITHER BETTER NOR WORSE?
THE FLOWERING BRANCHES GROW
NATURALLY, SOME LONG, SOME SHORT

DISTANCE AND MOBILITY

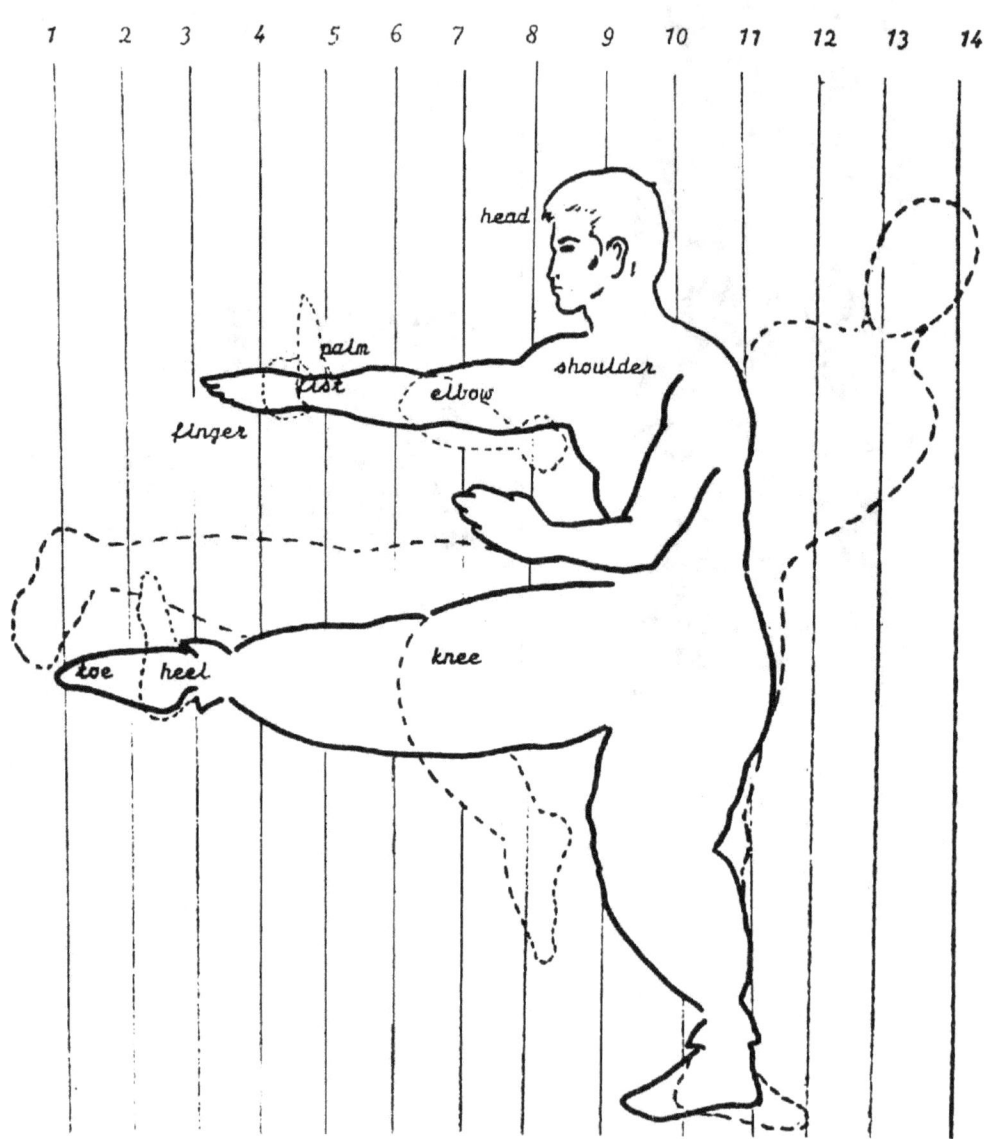

Weapons' Range:—using the longest against the nearest (check Progressive Target Chart)

Distance in fighting can be defined as the spatial relationship existing between two opponents. This spatial relationship will at any given time fall into one of three basic distances: long range, medium range, or close range. The fighter who can control the distance can usually control the fight, and whoever can control the fight stands a much better chance of winning. Therefore, in a fight, this spatial relationship is shifting and changing constantly as each fighter tries to outsmart the other and (1) find the correct distance to launch an attack; (2) cause the opponent's attacks to miss; and (3) disturb the opponent's plan of action. Which weapon you choose to attack with any particular moment is partially dependent upon what range you are in. Certain weapons can be used at all three ranges, others only one or two. For example, you wouldn't want to try and throw a close range weapon such as an elbow into the opponent's face while still at kicking range. You would seek to break the distance first. Likewise, you wouldn't attempt to use an extended, long range kicking attack while in punching range.

The distance one tries to maintain against the opponent is known as the "fighting measure." This "measure" is governed by several factors:

1. The maximum reach that can be attained with full extension for punching and striking weapons.
2. The reach of the opponent's weapons.
3. The amount of target one has to defend and what tools the opponent or both of you are allowed to use. For example, in boxing, no kicking attacks are allowed, so distance is adjusted to be concerned only with punching attacks at the upper body.

In kickboxing, the measure has to be expanded due to the fact that kicking and low line attacks are now part of one's arsenal and the whole body is a target.

Therefore, the distance you try to maintain is such that the opponent cannot land a hit against you without taking a step forward. This is known as the "brim of fire" line. And that plus a small step places you within hitting range.

1. High line attack distance.

2. Low line attack distance.

The ability to use distance to one's best advantage in both attack and defense requires:

1. Excellent footwork and mobility skills (smooth, fast, constant variety).
2. Precise evaluation of your own distance of attack and defense (length of weapons).
3. Evaluation of opponent's distance of attack (length of opponent's weapons, footwork, etc.).

Another reason for the continual gaining and breaking of distance is that any time you are in range to hit the opponent you are usually in range to be hit yourself. By making it more difficult for the opponent to be sure when you are in range for his attack, you gain an added safety factor.

Distance can be adjusted with:

1. Footwork—As opponent steps forward with his attack, break the distance with a push shuffle retreat (see *JKD Kickboxing*), ending just outside of opponent's punch.

2. Body sway—As opponent steps forward with his attack, his partner snaps back from the waist to increase the distance.

This may be necessary due to an inability to use footwork at that particular moment, but it is better to shift backward with footwork than over leaning backward because unless you are faster than your opponent, the sway leaves you open to his rear cross.

3. A combination of both footwork and body sway can also be used.

Distance varies with each opponent, and must be evaluated in regards to that individual. You must learn to be aware of the opponent's distance of attack and try to prevent him from coming into that distance. A tall fighter will usually try to keep a longer distance to use his reach with maximum effectiveness, and avoid the possibility of getting his limbs entangled and tied up in close. A shorter fighter must try to close the distance to be able to attack without being stopped by his opponent and held at bay in a range which may be detrimental. The key to successful distance is good footwork.

DISTANCE IN ATTACK

The three basic distances are as follows:
1. Long—kicks and long range punching.

2. Medium—medium range kicks, punches, knees.

3. Close—use of hooking blows, elbows, knees and other in-fighting techniques.

The first principle of distance is in using the longest weapon to hit the closest target:

1. Kicking—leading shin/knee side kick (with lean for added safety).

2. Striking—finger jab to eyes.

DISTANCE IN ATTACK

Your attack should be aimed at the distance the opponent will be at when he realizes he is being attacked and attempts to escape, parry or counter, not at the distance he is prior to the attack.

1. Incorrect gauge of distance—The attack is aimed to reach full extension at the point where the opponent's chin is prior to the attack. Just by the opponent shifting back slightly the attack falls short of its target.

2. Correct gauge of distance—By aiming the attack several inches past the opponent's chin while in the starting position, should the opponent step backwards slightly, the attack will land.

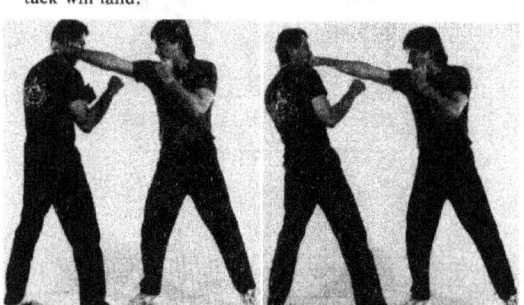

NOTE! Ascertaining the opponent's possible reactions to an attack through the use to feints and false attacks is integral in evaluating proper attacking distance. Does the opponent shift backward or attempt to crash forward and counter, etc.?

DISTANCE IN DEFENSE

1. When using distance in parry—A simple parry is best performed just as the opponent is at the end of his attacking action. If the parry is made just as the blow is about to land, the opponent will have little chance to counter your parry, and you will be in much better range to counter yourself.

a. Incorrect gauge of distance—By parrying too far away the defender opens the possibility of the attacker switching to another line of attack and is too far away to counterpunch.

b. Correct gauge of distance—By waiting until the last possible instant to parry, the defender is in a much tighter and safer position in which to counterpunch.

2. In parrying a combination attack—The rear foot should move with the first parry and the lead foot moves with second or remaining parries.

Against a jab-rear cross combination, the defender retreats with his rear foot while catching the jab, and pulls the lead foot back as he shoulder deflects the rear cross.

BREAKING OPPONENT'S DISTANCE

1. Creating a false sense of distance—You can create a false sense of distance in your opponent's defense by firing a weapon that by design falls short of the target. Although it appears to your opponent to be a full extension hit, it really isn't. This concept is shown in the following examples:

a. Short jab to extended jab—You can create a false sense of distance by throwing a jab without extending your shoulder. This may cause your opponent to feel that you can not hit him with a jab from that range. You can then score by firing a second jab while extending your shoulder.

b. Short cross to extended jab—This is another example of what Bruce Lee called throwing garbage to set up a powerful hit. This is the same principle as (a) above. In this case a short cross is thrown to create a false sense of distance, followed by an extended jab.

Creating a false sense of distance is good strategy if your opponent is not too aggressive but elusive.

2. Stealing a Step—
   a. Foot to hand—

You set this up by first throwing a fast powerful shin kick. If your opponent retreats

you can, in a sense, steal a step by faking a shin kick then stepping forward as your kicking foot descends putting you in hand range.

b. Jab to jab—
Jab then quickly step forward and hit with a second jab.

TRAINING AIDS FOR DISTANCE

1. The Mirror Footwork Drill—

In this exercise, two students face each other in an on-guard position. One partner leads the exercise by using different footwork motions. The partner mirror images the motion and attempts to maintain a specific and constant distance. For example:

Partners square off

as partner leading the exercise sidesteps to his right, the partner sidesteps left.

The first man then steps through with his left foot. His partner mirrors the motion by dropping his right foot back.

79

The first man now retreats with a step-slide, and his partner advances with a step-slide.

The above drill can be practiced at long, medium, and close range. The essence is to maintain a precise distance with your opponent while moving. For example, the man who initiates the movement acts as an attacker and tries to get in range so he can touch his partner with hand while the partner tries to stay outside of the brim of fire line.

2. Lunging Practice

This exercise aids in developing an explosive lunge which can be used to bridge the gap in attack:

Partner holds a sheet of paper about 18 inches beyond your extended finger jab position. Then from a basic on-guard position (arm retracted) explode with a finger jab aiming through the paper.

Once you feel comfortable doing this, have your partner retreat as he senses your hit. Like a lot of the drills, have fun and make a game out of it.

3. Attacking Drills Shifting From—

a. Hand to foot—After the student fires a punching combination, the trainer shifts out to kicking range. The student immediately adapts to the new distance and responds with a kicking attack.

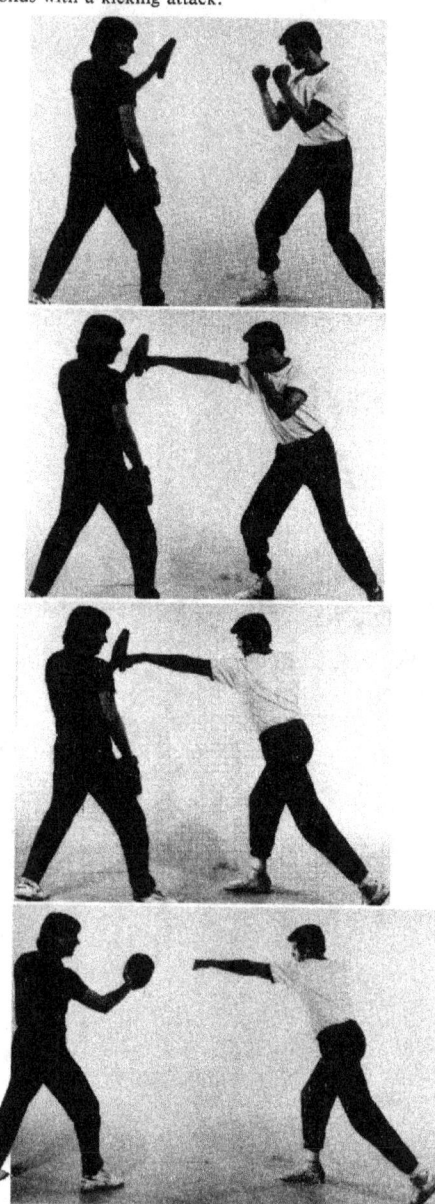

80

Below, the trainer feeds a low kick—

b. Foot to hand—

The student enters from kicking range and follows up as the trainer sets a punching combination.

4. Shadow Closing for Attack Drill: (sim. to mirror drill)

One man (A) moves forward and tries to bridge the gap (to get into hand range) but fires no hand or foot as this is just a footwork and distance drill.

The other man (B) who is acting as trainer retreats with step shuffle, slide shuffle, step and slide shuffle, or step back footwork.

A then follows like a shadow, not letting B widen the distance.

After A feels comfortable with this, B adds the following:
1. Angle right and left
2. Stopping
3. Stopping and moving again
4. Circling
5. Dropping to the floor

Also do shadow closing with the trainer holding a kicking shield or wearing focus gloves. With equipment you try and make contact while the trainer tries to stay out of range.

5. Hook Kick to Trap and Hit Distance Drill

In this drill the defender acts as the trainer by giving three different distances.

a. Stationary:

As you bridge the gap with a hook kick your training partner remains stationary. You then step straight down as you trap and hit.

b. Slide Back:

As you hook kick, your training partner slides back out of kicking range. By placing your kicking foot forward, you will be in range to trap and hit.

c. Step Back:

This is the same as (b) above, but when you kick your partner steps back.

d. Mix—When you have mastered the above, have your partner vary his responses while you flow.

6. Swinging a heavy bag or a hanging ball:

This is a good drill for distance and mobility. You simply swing a heavy bag or ball that you hang and try to maintain the proper fighting measure as it swings back and forth.

7. Shin Pad Drill:

While there are many Jun Fan shin pad drills, this is a simple one and also one of the most valuable. In this drill you attempt to side kick the shin of your training partner, who is wearing hockey or baseball type shin pads so you can really make contact, tries to avoid the kick. This is first done from a stationary position. Then while moving. Your partner can then give you different environments. For example:

He can:
 1. Step back
 2. Shuffle back
 3. Angle right or left
 4. Slide back. Then quickly move in.
 5. Move forward so you can practice the stop kick.

You simply relate to what your partner does.

ATTACK

An attack is an offensive action made with the objective of scoring a hit on an opponent. This action may be a single motion (simple attack) or compromised of several motions (compound/combination attack). It may be a direct attack in that it travels straight to the target via the most direct route. Or it may be indirect in which case while the attack begins in one line, it finishes in another.

The type of attack one uses is generally dictated by the form of defense used by the opponent. Is he a runner? Does he attempt to parry or does he attack into your attack? Likewise, the decision to use a particular offensive action is influenced by the opponent's technique and method of fighting (his on-guard position, the way he moves, his size, etc.). This is what Bruce meant when he stated, "My opponent's technique decides my techniques."

A main factor in attack is to try to take advantage of the opponent's weaknesses while avoiding his strengths. For example, if a man is a good kicker, when you stay out at long range you allow him to function in his area of strength. If you can close the distance and jam his kicking abilities, you avoid his strength. On the other hand, if the opponent is weak in grappling skills, you may seek to attack that area.

In Jun Fan there are five ways of attack:

1. Single Direct Attack—From an on-guard position the attacker shoots a punch directly to the opponent's midsection with no attempt to disguise the motion.

1a. Single Angulated Attack—From an on-guard position the attacker uses a direct attack but angles it with the use of footwork or body angulation.

2. Attack by Combination—The attacker bridges the gap with a low line kick, and follows up with a high backfist, low cross, lead uppercut punching combination.

84

4. Attack by Drawing—The attacker baits the opponent by appearing to lower his rear guard, then as the opponent kicks into the open line, the attacker angles his body and scores into the now open line.

3. Progressive Indirect Attack—The attacker draws a preliminary reaction from the opponent by using a low cross false attack to close the distance. The attacker then deceives the reaction and scores in an open line.

5. Hand Immobilization Attack—The attacker fires a lead punch to gain an attachment. He then immobilizes the arm and scores.

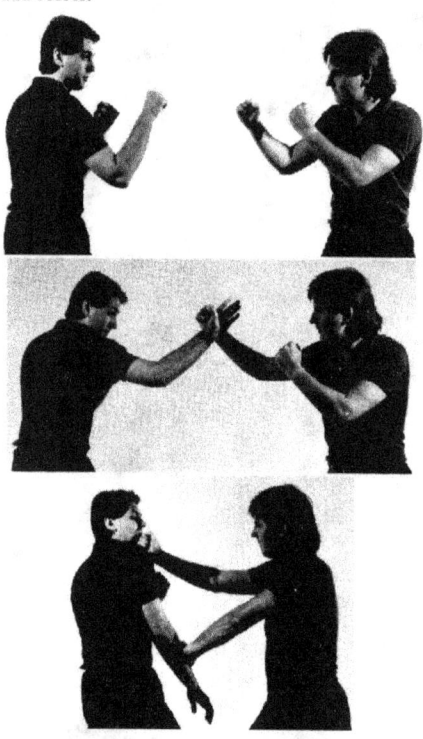

NOTE: For more detailed descriptions and examples of the five ways of attack refer to *Jeet Kune Do Kickboxing*.

PRIMARY/SECONDARY ATTACKS

(A) Primary attacks are offensive actions initiated by oneself with the intention of landing using:

1. PACE—Using one's superior speed and accuracy with no attempt to disguise the attack.

    For example: From an on-guard position the attacker closes the distance and lands a lead side kick to the opponent's lead knee.

2. FRAUD—To deceive the opponent by appearing to attack in one particular line and upon drawing a reaction switching the attack to hit in an open line.

    For example: The attacker fires a straight punch, drawing a lead hand cross parry from the opponent. Before the parry touches, the attacker evades the parry and scores with a rear cross to the open line.

3. FORCE—Attacking a closed line with sufficient force to open it.

For example: The attacker uses a lead hand beat to open the opponent's line just enough to enter with a lead punch while covering opponent's lead arm with tan sao.

(B) Secondary attacks are offensive actions intended to outmaneuver or retaliate against the attacks initiated by the opponent in one or another of their different stages:

1. Attack on the Preparation—A preparation is any preliminary movement a fighter makes to facilitate the development of his offensive action such as taking a step forward, or attempting to engage the opponent's arm. Such motions are sometimes referred to as "motions without intention" in that there is no actual offensive action involved. An attack on preparation must be done before the opponent starts his attack. Split-second timing differentiates between attack on preparation and counterattack. The attacking action you use against the opponent's preparation should be as simple as possible to give the opponent the least amount of time to reorganize.

2. Attack on Development—An attacking action that arrests the opponent's action midway to the target.

3. Attack on Completion—An attacking action made as the opponent's action is at full extension.

NOTE: For photo sequences refer to Chapter 6—"Timing and Rhythm."

SIMPLE ATTACK

A simple attack is a single offensive action executed in one tempo with the objective of going to the target via the most direct route. Single Direct Attack and Single Angulated Attack would be classified as simple attacks. Simple attacks are classified in two categories: 1. Direct and 2. Indirect.

A direct attack is made into the line of engagement or an opposite line by simply "beating the opponent to the punch" or catching his moment of vulnerability. Direct attack should be timed against the opponent's:

1. Absence of Touch—From an on-guard position without attachment the attacker scores with his lead punch.

2. Engagement—From a position of attachment the attacker shoots a lead punch and scores.

3. Change of Engagement—From a high reference attachment, as the opponent attempts to shift to a low line engagement the attacker scores with a straight while also covering opponent's change of engagement.

Direct Attack should also be practiced against any of the above combined with a step forward.

Indirect Attack is a single movement, the first half of which causes some reaction from the opponent so that the second half of the motion may be completed opposite the original line of engagement into an open line.

Indirect Attack with disengagement should be practiced against opponent's:

1. Beat—As the opponent attempts to use a lead hand beat to open your line, you disengage to the inside using jao sao before the beat touches, and score in the open line with a backfist while trapping the opponent's arm for added safety.

2. Engagement—As the opponent attempts to engage your lead arm in high outside reference point, you disengage to the inside high line with a jao sao and score with a finger jab while simultaneously checking the opponent's lead arm for added safety.

3. Change of Engagement—From a low outside reference point, as the opponent attempts to switch to a high reference point, you disengage using jao sao to the inside line and score with a high extended palm hook.

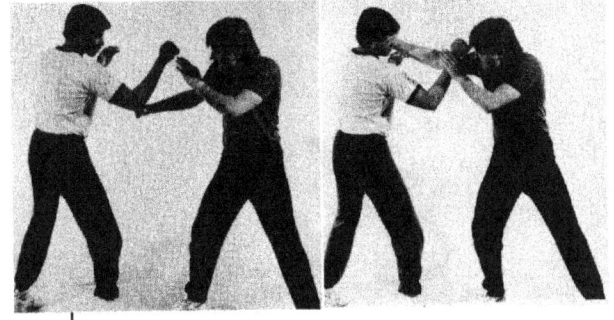

Indirect Attack with disengagement should also be practiced against any of the above combined with a step forward.

COMPOUND/COMBINATION ATTACKS

A compound attack is an offensive action that includes one or more feints before the final hit. A combination attack is comprised of several offensive actions each of which is intended to land. In both forms the attacking motions flow from one to another naturally, and are usually thrown to more than one target area. Progressive Indirect Attack is an example of a compound attack, whereas Attack by Combination would be a combination attack.

When using either a compound or combination attack two basic factors need to be evaluated in regards to the particular combination of weapons used.

These two factors are:

1. Using movements that are most economical for yourself. By using movements that don't require extreme changes in the on-guard position and major preparatory motions, you reduce the risk of being countered.

2. Using movements that are the most direct to the opponent in light of "between" combinations of kicking tools and striking tools. Knowing which strikes "fit" together naturally and smoothly without major gaps during which the opponent can escape or counter hit.

Therefore, train yourself to examine all combinations in terms of:

a. Facilitating a speedy recovery to the on-guard position.

b. Being able to attack and defend from where you end up or are going to end up.

Short, Fast/Deep, Penetrative Combinations:

In attack you may use a short, fast combination if you are in close,

or a deep, penetrative (still fast) combination if the range is greater.

TIMING THE ATTACK

The right time to attack is when your opponent is not able to use distance to his advantage and is therefore forced to parry your attack, or when your opponent makes the initial movement of his front foot in the step forward and it is impossible for him to suddenly change his mind.

There are two basic moments for attack:

1. When your own will decides the time to attack.
2. When it depends upon the opponent's movements or the failure of his actions.

By preliminary probing we can ascertain the opponent's reactions—whether or not he uses distance, parries hard, tries to crash, etc., and then decide, without a moment's hesitation, the best type of attack to accomplish the job. Once we have this information and are ready to attack, the following factors will increase the chances for success:

1. Estimate the correct distance so your attack lands precisely on target and not too short or too far. (See distance in Attack.)
2. Time your attack properly to catch the opponent in a moment of unpreparedness and regulate the speed of the attack to the speed of the opponent. In this way your attack will be "on time" (see Timing) and neither too fast nor too slow.
3. Maintain a loose "pliable" awareness—constantly watching the opponent and being alert to the opponent's attempts to stop hit, counterattack, etc.
4. Try to keep the proper degree of relaxation in the muscles to be used so you can explode with your attack. If you're too tense you will move slower—so try to stay loose.

In order to reduce the risk of the opponent stop-hitting or countering you in the midst of your attack you should:

1. Maintain a well-covered position in attack.
2. Fire the weapon straight from the neutral ready position without telegraphing your intentions by winding up, pulling back, etc. In other words, kick or strike without preparation.
3. Recover immediately to either:
   a. Continue the attack.
   b. Defend if necessary.

MINOR VS. MAJOR BLOWS

In boxing, the lead jab is not designed to knock an opponent out. Rather it is designed to set the range, offset the opponent, and set up the combinations of finishing blows. It is a minor blow, *not* in terms of the extent of its use, but in terms of overall power. Minor blows can be described as those which are not ordinarily used as knockout or finishing blows. Minor blows are generally used for the following purposes:

1. To irritate and offset the opponent as he prepares to launch his attack. For example, a low kick to opponent's calf to irritate.

2. To set up a finishing blow by either opening a line, stunning momentarily, or affecting the opponent's balance. For example, a backhand flick.

3. To distract or offset the possibility of the opponent counterattacking in the midst of your attack.

Some strikes can be used as both minor and major blows. It depends upon the amount of force put behind the strike. For example:

1. Here is a straight right being used more to offset an opponent or set up another attack.

2. Here is a straight being used as a finishing blow. Notice the full commitment of the fighter's body weight behind the blow as compared to the first photograph.

NEGATIVE AND POSITIVE ENERGY

Major and minor blows are both examples of positive energy blows in that energy is transferred from your strike to your opponent. With a major blow there is a lot of energy while there is less energy transferred with a minor blow. The less energy that is transferred to your opponent in your first strike, the faster the second strike will be. A negative energy strike is one in which little or no energy is transferred to your opponent. It differs from a feint in that it is intended to touch your opponent. A negative energy attack can be used for the following purposes:

1. To set up a finishing blow by opening a line.
2. As a "feeler" to probe your opponent's defenses without using much commitment.
3. As a range finder to feel the proper range for a more positive energy attack.

Below are two examples of a negative jab followed by a positive cross.

1. Holding a focus glove.

2. Wearing a focus glove.

NARROWING OPPONENT'S GUARD

You may seek to narrow an opponent's guard by using straight blows to draw the guard inwards and creating an opening for looping, hooking blows from the outside.

OPENING OPPONENT'S GUARD

You may alternately seek to open the opponent's guard through the use of wide hooking blows; then finish up with tight blows inside the opponent's now open guard.

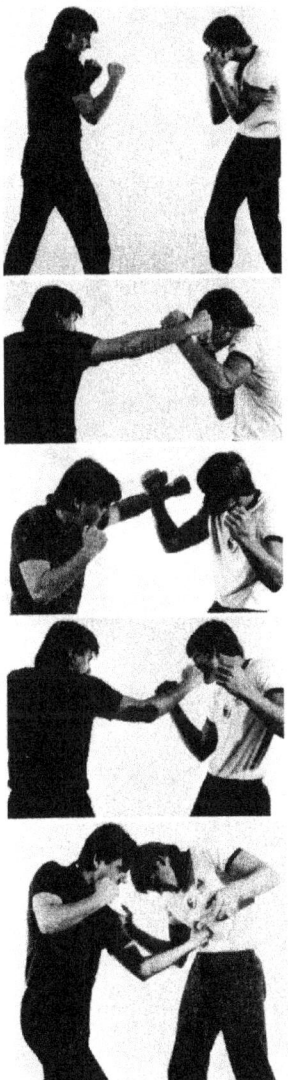

USE OF THE "BEAT" IN ATTACK

The term "beat" is from fencing. It is a sharp blow delivered crisply on the opponent's blade, and is used to either secure an opening into which an attack can travel or draw a reaction which can then be evaded and score in another line. In Jun Fan the attacker uses his own arm as if it were a sword and hits into the opponent's arm to achieve the same results. It is not a block.

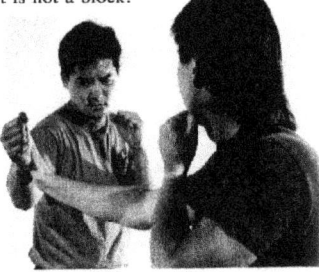

The Beat Used for Opening a Line: The beat is used against the inside of the opponent's arm to open the line so that the attacker's punch can score. (Note the attacker's rear guard checks the arm upon which the beat was made.)

The Beat Used for Drawing a Reaction: As the beat is made, the opponent reacts by blocking inwards in an attempt to re-close the line. As his arm is moving inwards the attacker disengages to the outside line, scores with a backfist while trapping the opponent's arm with his guarding hand.

The Beat as a Gauge of Distance: The beat can also be used to gauge distance. For example, when your opponent jabs, you lean back to avoid the punch, beat against his jab to gauge the proper distance while at the same time delivering a hook kick to the groin.

The Beat Used as a Distraction: The beat can also be used to distract your opponent to help facilitate your attack. For example, the attacker bridges the gap and beats the inside of his opponent's arm. Then hook kicks him in the groin.

Generally, the purpose of the beat is to provoke a split second delay in the opponent's reactions, thus allowing more time for the execution of the attacker's succeeding offensive actions, be it simple or compound. The beat can be done against the inside or outside of the opponent's arms.

THE THREE LEVELS OF ATTACK

The following are examples of Combination Attacks Bridging from Long Range and Using the Three Levels: high, medium, and low.

1. Bridge with low hook kick to knee, high backfist, knee to midsection.

2. Bridge the gap with low side kick, follow with middle lead punch, high rear hook.

3. Bridge the gap with inverted lead hook kick to middle line, follow with low side kick and high back hammerfist.

96

FEINTING

A feint is an offensive action aimed at diverting an opponent's attention from the real point of attack. Feinting is used primarily to make an opponent react, usually with a defensive motion, then to act upon his reaction while executing the final, real attack.

The primary objectives of feinting are:

1. To make the opponent hesitate while immediately closing the distance.

Here the attacker diverts his opponent's attention by using a low kick feint while simultaneously bridging the gap, then lands a high lead backfist, middle cross combination.

2. To open the line in which one intends to attack.

Here the attacker feints with a high lead to the opponent's outside line. As the opponent's lead arm moves outward to close the line, the attacker uses a jao sao to disengage to the inside line and complete his attack in the now open line.

Another example of this is to follow the lead hand feint with a rear sliding leverage hit to the inside line.

3. To deceive with the front hand so the rear hand can score. Attacker shoots lead finger jab, as opponent blocks outward, attacker fires rear finger jab inside.

Even if his front hand remains high you can score with a sliding leverage hit.

4. To deceive the parry which the feint provokes.
Here the attacker uses a low lead punch feint to draw the opponent's lead hand parry, which the attacker evades by firing a high rear cross over the downward moving arm.

The attacker uses the same low lead feint, but this time the opponent attempts to parry with his rear hand. The attacker deceives the parry by switching to a high lead hook attack.

5. To observe and ascertain the opponent's reactions.
Here the attacker fires a lead high jab feint to observe how the opponent reacts, in this case by retreating.

6. To draw a counter strike from the opponent which can then be countered.
Here the attacker feints a low lead to draw the opponent's rear cross counter which he counters by rolling away and firing a high lead hook to the opponent's face.

7. To set a body pattern, then giving a corresponding move to indicate the same pattern. Then change. Here are examples of a hand feint coordinated with a body fake.

a. Low jab to rear overhead. Set the feint up with a strong, positive low jab.

Then lower your body as you feint a low jab followed by a rear overhead.

b. Low jab to high hook. This is the same as above, but you follow the low feint with a high hook.

100

c. High jab to low uppercut. Set up the feint with a strong, positive high jab. Then feint the jab followed by a front uppercut to the body.

Feints can be divided into two categories:
1. Simple Feints—A single motion such as half-motion kick feint.
2. Compound Feints—Comprised of two or more feints used in conjunction. Compound feints can be used vertically (low feint/high feint—high feint/low feint), laterally (inside feint/outside feint), or using a combination of the two (low straight feint/high hook feint).

One important point to remember is that the more feints you utilize in your offensive action, the greater the chance that the opponent can counterattack you or escape out of range with a quick retreat. Therefore, usually keep feinting motions to a maximum of two at a time.

Make every feint action in a constant progression towards the target in order to emphasize the value of the feint. By combining the feint with an advance you can not only achieve this but also gain distance. A good feint must appear so real that the opponent is obliged to react. It must be decisive, expressive and threatening—yet at the same time seem to be a simple attacking movement. If the opponent can sense that it is an obvious fake he will not take the bait. Bruce Lee used to say that your feint should make your opponent feel "faint."

VARIOUS TYPES OF FEINTS

Feints can be made using a single limb, the body, footwork, or any combination of them. What type you use depends upon what reaction you wish to draw, range from the opponent, etc. The following photographs illustrate various types of feints. The feinting motion itself has been exaggerated slightly for the reader's clarity.

Arm Feints:

Upward feint.

Downward feint.

Drawback feint.

Inside or outside feint.

Lead arm swing feint.

Leg Feints:

Lift—a quick lifting of either leg.

Half motion kick—A small kicking motion at any of the low lines while maintaining a well-covered position.

Body Feints:

Knee feint. Quickly bend the lead knee, creating the feeling that the arms are moving as well.

102

Body drop feint. Quickly bend the upper body forward, while bending the knees and moving the rear hand forward.

Side bend feint. Drop the body to the left and forward while creating the impression of throwing a lead or a rear hand.

Arm and leg feints can be done with either the lead or rear arm or leg.

Feints should be used at all three levels when combining hand and foot attacks.

For example:
a. Feint kick low/hit high line.
b. Feint kick low/hit medium line.
c. Feint hit medium/kick high line.
d. Feint hit high/kick low.

The speed of one's feint must be regulated to the opponent's reaction speed. If you shift from the feint too quickly your attack may end up in a still closed line. If you hold the feint too long you may be counter hit by the opponent.

a. Too fast—By not waiting long enough for the desired reaction the attacker ends his attack in a closed line.

b. Too slow—By holding the feint too long the attacker is counter hit before he can switch his attack.

FALSE ATTACK

A false attack is different than a feint in that it is an attack that is intended to fall short of the target, yet travel deep enough to lure a reaction or ascertain the opponent's reaction (see negative energy).

Example:

Here a middle line lead punch is used as a false attack.

As opposed to a single attack which is intended to land.

The main purpose of false attacks is the use of Progressive Indirect Attack. After attacking a particular line with a single direct attack one or two times, the false attack is then used to allow a rapid shift to the alternate line of attack. Distance is extremely important. If you are too close you can be hit, and if you are too far the opponent won't fall for it.

THE DELAYED HIT

The delayed hit is good strategy against an opponent who overparries or remains stationary when punched.

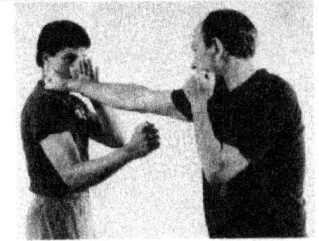

To do a delayed hit start a jab. Stop for a split second as your opponent parries. Then complete the jab on the other side of the parry. Don't retract the arm!

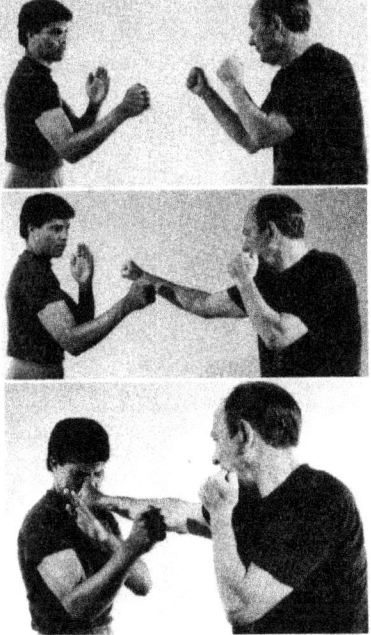

COUNTERTIME IN ATTACK

Countertime is an offensive action used after parrying, avoiding or escaping an opponent's counterattack. You attack with the idea of drawing a stop hit or time hit in a particular line in order to parry or avoid it and score. It differs from counterattack in that countertime is set up by the attacker. It also differs from Attack by Drawing in that you attack first with the intention of countering the opponent's counterattack.

Countertime can be very effective against an opponent whose game is built on counter offensive actions and who either continually tries to stop hit, or one who attacks into your attack. It requires cool anticipation of the opponent's counterattack (what line his counter will come in) and good timing.

Countertime can be used with various preparations such as feints, sudden advances, attacks on the arm to provoke a counterattack which can then be countered.

1. Feints—The attacker feints high to draw an anticipated lead hook counterattack which he then avoids and countertimes with his own rear cross.

2. Sudden advances—The attacker advances suddenly with a quick push shuffle, drawing the opponent's anticipated lead hook to the head, which he then countertimes with a high rear cross.

Attack on the Arm—The attacker uses an inside beat against the opponent to draw an anticipated lead hook which he then countertimes with a high rear cross.

Note that the preceding photo sequences all used the same countertime attack against the opponent's counter to the preparation. It is extremely important when you use countertime to maintain a well-covered position.

COUNTERTIME AGAINST VARIOUS BLOCKERS

1. The touch and go opponent.

Many martial artists will block and then quickly hit with the same hand.

Against this type of opponent you can:
  a. Parry and backfist.

  b. Parry and bicep hit to finger jab to descending trap to backhand chop (from Kali).

  c. You can parry and hit low.

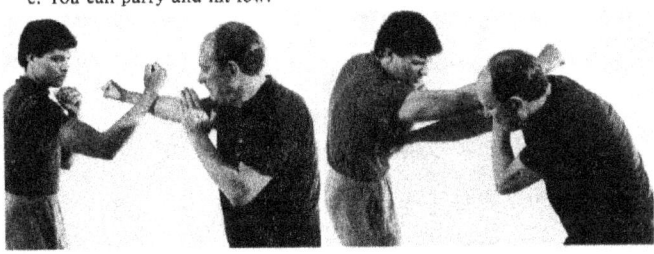

d. Or parry and hit high.

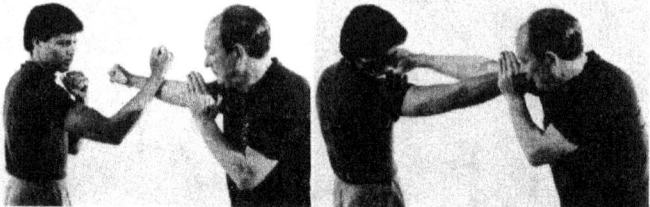

e. You can parry and hook kick groin.

2. The block and hit opponent.

Against such an opponent you can down parry with a simultaneous palm smash.

3. The opponent who uses distance then hits. When you side kick to the opponent's shin, he retreats then steps forward with a lead jab which you cross parry while hitting low.

4. The opponent who traps and hits.

As your opponent starts to trap, angle to the outside as you trap and hit.

5. Against the boxer who rolls away from a cross and returns a cross. As he crosses you cross parry with a simultaneous finger jab.

FLOWING FROM ONE MARTIAL ART TO ANOTHER IN ATTACK

In Jun Fan you should have the ability to flow from one martial art to another. As an example in Kali theory an attack consists of three elements: 1. Entering. 2. Follow-ups. 3. Finishing techniques. Notice these three elements in the following examples:

1. Jun Fan hook kick to Thai elbow to Silat inside foot sweep.

2. Savate round kick to Thai round kick to Kali up elbow to Thai knee to Kali head throw to Hsing-i palm smash.

110

3. Jun Fan shin kick to Kali oblique kick to Wing Chun trap and punch to boxing cross to body hook.

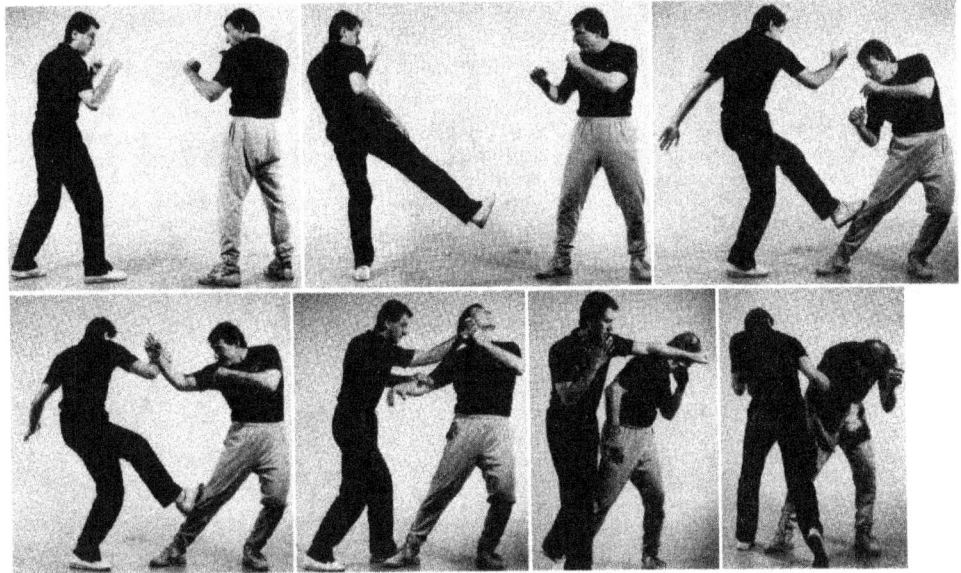

JUN FAN ENTRY ATTACKS

Below is a list of some of the Jun Fan entry attacks. Except for No. 2 we ask you to supply which hand and which foot to use at any particular time. Experiment as you play with these bridging the gap techniques.

1. High hand to low foot to high hand.
2. High hand with low foot (at the same time)—finger jab with leg obstruction shin kick.
3. Low foot to high hand.
4. High hand to low hand.
5. High hand to low hand to high hand.
6. Low hand to high hand.
7. Low hand to high hand to low hand.
8. Low hand to high hand to low foot.
9. Foot to low hand.
10. High hand to high hand to low foot.

Most of these can be done as a PIA attack, an ABC attack or as an ABC with Broken Rhythm (see Chapter 6).

COUNTERATTACK

Counterattack can be defined as an offensive or defensive-offensive action executed against the opponent's attack. The difference between counterattack and countertime again is that in counterattack the opponent initiates the action whereas in countertime you do.

Offensive counterattack—Stop hit/kick
Defensive-offensive counterattack—
Time hit/kick
Parry and hit/kick

THE STOP HIT/KICK

The stop hit or kick is an offensive motion. It is not just sticking out an arm or leg and allowing the opponent to run into it when they attack. The stop hit or kick must land before the opponent's final action and requires excellent judgment, precise timing and correct distance. Therefore it should be used sparingly, otherwise the opponent can draw your stop hit and counter it. Used judiciously and correctly, it can be extremely effective against an opponent who prepares for an attack with a step forward or attacks with feints and wide attacking actions.

1. Defender uses a lead side stop kick as opponent steps forward to prepare to attack.

2. Defender uses an angulated lead jab stop hit against attacker's wide lead hook.

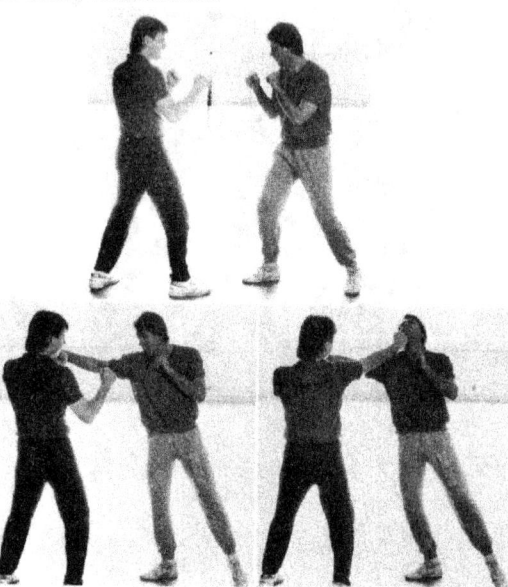

The risk factor in using a stop hit becomes greater as the opponent's attack is developed further. A stop hit/kick may also be combined with footwork to secure the best distance.

You may use a stop hit with: a. advance; b. retreat; c. angulation; d. stationary.

Examples of Stop Hits/Kicks

1. Using a lead jab as a stop hit against the opponent's lead hand attack.

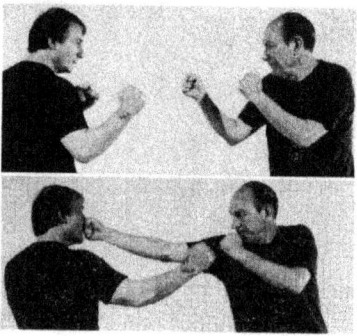

2. Using a lead jab as a stop hit against the opponent's lead kick attack.

3. Using a lead side stop kick against the opponent's lead kick attack.

4. Using a lead side stop kick against the opponent's lead hand attack.

STOP HIT/KICK DRILLS

Below is a sample of progressive drills to train the stop hit or kick. To do these drills the trainer should wear boxing gloves, body armor, head gear, and shin pads, while the student wears boxing gloves. It is through drilling that you develop technique.

 a. Trainer—initiates a hand or foot attack. Defender—stop hits or kicks.

 b. Trainer—initiates any kick. Defender—stop hit or kick.

 c. Trainer—initiates any two kicks. Defender—uses distance against first kick, stop hit or kick on trainer's second kick.

 d. Trainer—initiates jab. Defender—uses any counter kick as a stop kick.

 e. Trainer—uses any hand attack. Defender—uses 1. only stop kicks; 2. only stop hits; 3. uses stop hit or kick.

 f. Trainer—uses any hand or foot. Defender—stop hits or kicks—evades—stop hits or kicks.

THE TIME HIT/KICK

A time hit/kick is a stop hit which lands while at the same time preventing the opponent's attack from arriving on target. It anticipates the line in which the attack will end, then closes the line so as to hit the opponent while carrying the opponent's attacking limb clear. It is literally a stop hit while closing the line of attack.

Time-hitting requires: 1. correct anticipation of the opponent's attacking intentions; 2. precise placing of the tool in the path of the final movement of attack; and 3. precision in hitting the available target. If you try to time-hit too soon the opponent can switch his line of attack, and if you wait too long the opponent can score.

Examples of Time-Hitting

1. Against the opponent's lead hand attack, the defender uses a rear hand outside sliding leverage hit to both deflect the attack and score.

2. Against the opponent's lead hand attack, the defender uses a rear hand inside sliding leverage hit to deflect the attack and score.

THE SINGLE TIME-HIT—Simultaneous block and hit.
  Examples of single time-hit:
  1. Parry and punch to inside line against jab.

2. Tan with punch against jab.

114

THE RESPONSE HIT is a counterattack where you parry and attack an opponent before his attacking limb has recovered his guard. Usually used against a hand attack. For example:

Catch your opponent's jab then hit him with a cross before he returns to an on-guard position.

DOUBLE TIME

In a double time counterattack you parry and then hit. In Jun Fan this is usually against a kicking attack or with a beat against a hand attack. Example of double time with a beat against a jab.

Of course in combat you don't tell yourself that you're going to do a stop hit, or a single time-hit, or a double time-hit, etc. You merely relate to your opponent and try to act as efficiently as possible. Which one of the above is the most efficient? Which one is the least efficient? What kind of follow-ups can you use after each one?

JAMMING

Jamming can also be used to offset the opponent's attack and put you in position to counterattack. When you jam an attack you crash into the attacking line in a well-covered position, nullifying the attack and putting you in position to shift to close range fighting or to shove your opponent out to kicking range. For example, the defender detects the attacker's kick as it starts and slides in to jam the attack.

Make sure you are in a balanced position when you jam to avoid being knocked over.

USE OF THE PARRY IN COUNTERATTACK

The parry is a defensive motion used to deflect an opponent's attack in its attempt to reach the target. Like attacks, and counterattacks, you have simple parries and compound or combination parries. The defensive parry should halt as soon as the attack is blocked. If not, it gives an extra 'push' to the opponent's tool which he may be able to use to his advantage by switching the attack into another line. Consider parrying as 'closing' the door on an attack as opposed to 'slamming' it shut.

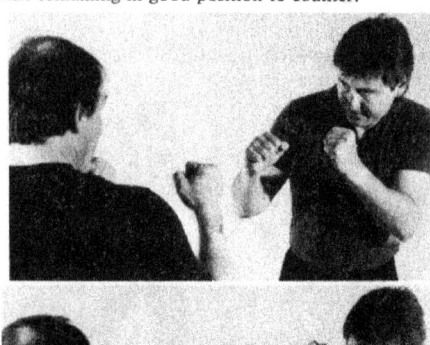

1. Good Parry—The defender has diverted the attack while remaining in good position to counter.

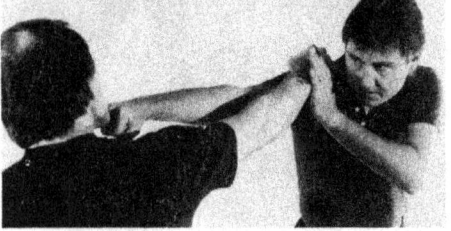

2. Over Parry—By parrying too hard the defender has knocked the attacker's arm into his own, destroying his ability to counter with that arm.

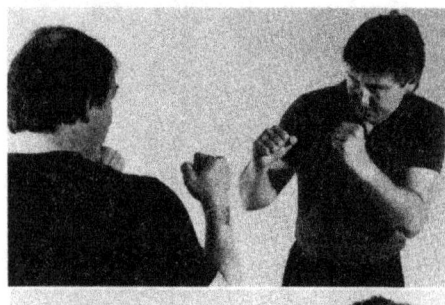

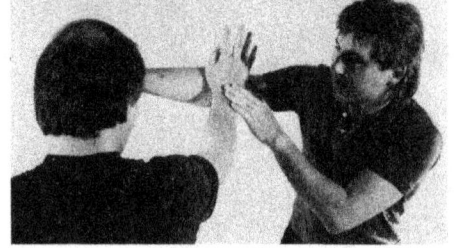

3. Under Parry—By not parrying sufficiently the defender has allowed the attacker's punch to still land.

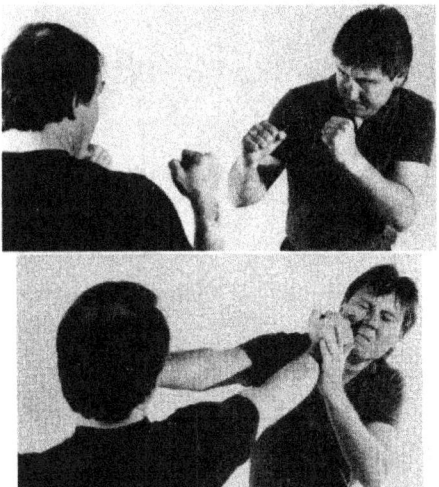

Parrying can be made more efficient by including body positioning such as a slight lean or footwork such as side-stepping with it. When fighting an opponent who has superior skill or has a reach advantage, one may need to take a backward step when making the parry as opposed to drawing the arm back. This action helps you maintain a "buffer zone" between you and the opponent, and needs to be adjusted to the length of the opponent's attacking movement to ensure the required distance is maintained for a successful counterattack. When using multiple parries, each should be made smoothly and controlled, so that the succeeding parry can be executed with maximum speed and firmness. The final parry should not be made too soon, to avoid giving the opponent the chance to deceive it. In this example, the defender reaches too far forward to try to parry, allowing the attacker to switch his attack and score.

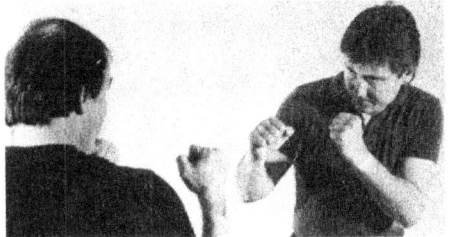

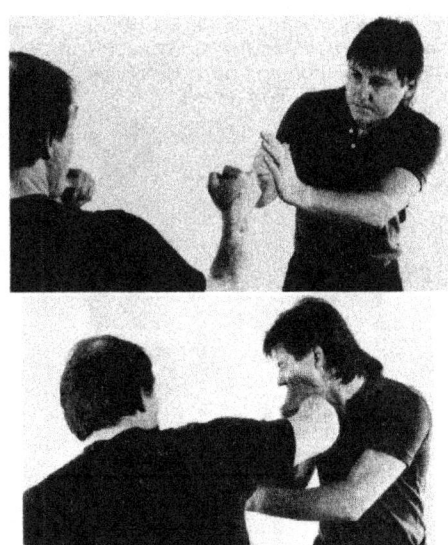

Semicircular Parries

These are parries taken from either the low line to the high line, or the high line to the low line in which the parrying motion describes a half circle. Semicircular parries can be used against a shifting attack that is made on the same side of the body. They can be done with either the lead or rear hand.

Examples:

1. As the attacker fires a high long lead hook, the defender covers the line with tan sao, then as the attacker shifts to a low hooking attack the defender uses a semicircular parry, while scoring with his own lead punch.

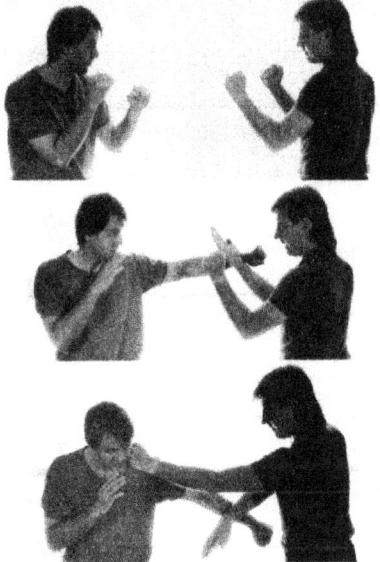

2. As the attacker finds his low lead attack parried by the defender's lead arm, he switches to a high backfist which the defender counters by using a low to high lead semicircular parry, and scores with his rear punch.

A counter-hit may be inserted in between the parries or one may counterattack after having made the deflection. If one is caught unaware one may have to use the parry with a retreat also, depending upon the attacker's motion.

Circular Parries

A circular parry envelops the attacker's arm and brings it back to the original line of engagement. It should be a small motion that sweeps the attacker's arm clear of the target, and requires excellent timing and sensitivity.

Examples:

1. Against a high outside reference point, as the attacker attempts to jao sao to the high inside line, the defender uses a clockwise circular parry to bring the attacker's arm back to its original outside line.

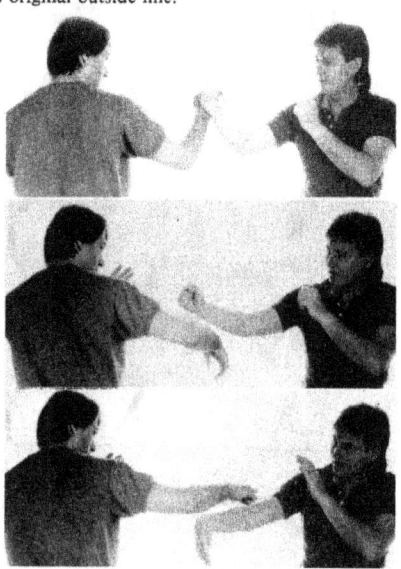

2. In an unmatched lead and against a high inside reference point, as the attacker attempts to jao sao to the outside line, the defender uses a counterclockwise circular parry to bring the attacker's arm back to its original inside line.

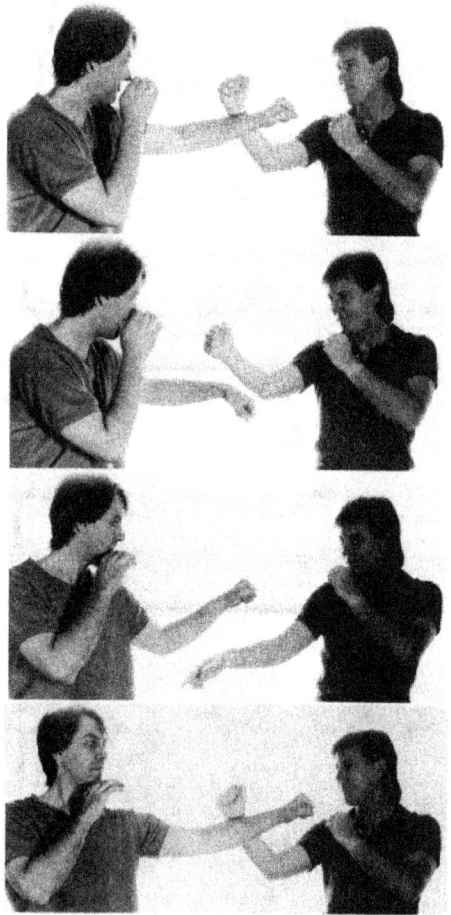

As with the semicircular parry examples, the circular parries have been shown strictly as defensive movement without hits for the sake of clarity.

In this example we have taken the previous sequence of photographs and the defender uses an outside sliding leverage hit at the end.

Sometimes in parrying an attack the hand detaches from the opponent's arm after the parry in order to change to another form of attack.

For example, here the defender parries opponent's lead jab while sidestepping and then fires a lead hook kick to groin.

Other times the defender maintains the parry in order to trap or immobilize the arm.

For example, here the defender parries opponent's lead attack but maintains attachment as he uses a jao sao to jut sao combination.

In consideration of countering, three factors must be analyzed and understood: 1. The lead of the opponent. This is important in that it determines the portion of the body open to counterattack.

a. A lead attack exposes the lead side of the body.

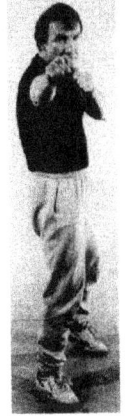 

b. A rear attack exposes almost all of opponent's torso.

2. Whether the counterattack should be one or two handed.

a. Blocking, guarding, stopping and parrying leave one hand with which to counter. Defender uses lead hand to cross parry, while scoring with a low rear cross.

b. Slipping, sidestepping, ducking, bob and weaving all allow two hand counters. Defender slips inside lead attack and counters with lead body hook.

3. Counter blow depends upon method of avoiding opponent's lead as well as the lead itself. a. Defender slips inside lead attack and counter punches with a rear body hook.

b. Defender sidesteps outside lead attack and counter kicks with lead hook kick.

c. Defender ducks under rear attack and counters with grappling.

DEFENSE AGAINST COUNTERATTACKS

The best defense against counterattacks is basically to give the opponent as little opportunity as possible to use them.

Offensively, the best tactics are: 1. Using mainly simple attacks to offset the validity of counterattacks. 2. Avoid overly complex attacks. 3. Be prepared automatically to offset any counterattack.

Defensively the best tactic is second intention using counter time, that is, an offensive action that follows the parrying of a counterattack.

To minimize the risk of counterattack you should:

1. Feint to disturb your opponent's rhythm, offset him and cause him to lose movement in time.

2. Change your body position during your attack by slipping, changing levels, having an elusive head, and other evasive body actions.

3. Constantly vary your attacks and defense to make it difficult for an opponent to 'read' you.

DEFENSE

Defense can be defined as protection from or resistance against attacks. The basic forms of defense utilized in Jun Fan are:
1. Distance
2. Blocking and Hitting
3. Parrying and Hitting
4. Evasiveness
5. Intercepting

For an in-depth view of these defensive skills refer to *JKD Kickboxing*.

Here we want to deal with one specific form of defense—evasion. Sooner or later it may become necessary to evade an attack, when for some reason you are not in position to counter or are caught unaware, or the opponent is faster or stronger, and you find yourself in the position of having to evade his attack.

Evasion can be accomplished with:
1. Footwork—sidestepping
           retreat step
           angle step
2. Body motion—slipping   ducking
           bob and weave   snap back
3. Combination of above—45 degree shift
   shoulder roll with footwork

TRAINING DRILLS FOR EVASIVENESS

The following drills are included in the Jun Fan curriculum to help the student increase his abilities to evade an opponent.

1. One partner stands with his rear foot near a wall and is only allowed to use lateral footwork movement and upper body evasions against the feeder who throws various punches and kicks which the defender must evade. (The feeder is at a designated range and is not allowed to crash in during this drill.)

2. Same as above only this time the defender is placed in a corner, allowing only 90 degrees of movement.

3. Both partners are moving with each other; one man is all offense and his partner is allowed to use defensive skills including parrying.

NOTE: These training drills are exactly that, *Training Drills*. They have to be done honestly and realistically, because it is a known fact that if someone throws enough attacks at you, eventually some are going to land. The essence of the drills are twofold in purpose. While one man develops his evasive skills, the partner is refining his attack skills. The speed must be regulated to allow the defender to develop his skills, and is progressively increased as the student's evasive skills improve.

4. Charlo's Training Drill—In this drill the trainer stands stationary with both arms extended at shoulder level. The partner then practices shifting from outside to inside position while punching. At the inside position he shifts from close range back to long range while punching, then shifts back to inside and bob and weaves to outside. The main idea is to not stop and work on being as evasive as possible.

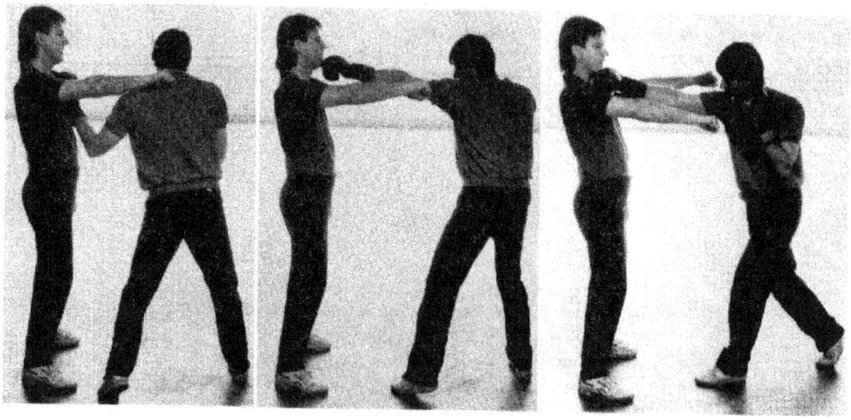

124

TIMING AND RHYTHM

You may have the best technique in the world, or the greatest speed, but if you don't understand timing, or have poor timing, your chances of success are lowered. Timing means the ability to recognize the right moment and seize the opportunity for an action. This moment may be seized instinctively as it occurs naturally, or provoked consciously by an action, and must be sensed rather than perceived. Timing and speed are complementary. (See section on "Speed" to cross-relate.)

Timing can be broken down into two types:
1. Reaction Time
2. Movement Time

REACTION TIME

Total reaction time consists of three elements:
1. Time required for a stimulus to reach the receivers. We may hear it (audio), see it (visual) or feel it (tactile).
2. Plus the time required for the brain to relay the impulses through the proper nerve fibers to the proper muscles.
3. The time to get the appropriate muscles into action after receiving the impulse.

If one were to chart an example of the time to complete a response, it would look like this:

```
Presentation of       Beginning          End of
   Stimulus          of Movement        Movement
*_____*_____*
*_____*
                    Response Time
```

An individual's reaction time can become longer under the following conditions:
1. Lack of training in any system.
2. Tiredness (physical or mental).
3. Loss of proper focus, lack of concentration, etc.
4. Emotional upheavals (anger, fear, etc.).

LENGTHENING THE OPPONENT'S REACTION TIME

What you seek to do is to catch the opponent either physically or mentally unaware, or create a situation in which he is unable to react with a controlled action to your attack thereby forcing him to move involuntarily and without premeditation. Some excellent times to attack during which the opponent's reaction time is increased are:
1. Immediately after he completes a technique.
2. When he is concerned with multiple stimuli.
3. As he inhales.
4. When he withdraws his energy (involves attitude).
5. When his attention has been diverted.
6. When he's physically or mentally off balance.

TRAINING FOR REACTION TIME IMPROVEMENT

(As speed and timing are complementary, cross-reference these training guides with the section on reaction speed.) The time it takes to discern an attack coming usually consumes the greater part of total reaction time. There are two main ways of reducing it:
1. Develop your abilities to grasp and "keep" the object in your field of vision beforehand, as well as developing the ability to foresee beforehand all the possible movements of the attacking weapon. The first part means that you should train yourself to never lose sight of the opponent's arms or legs if possible. (In boxing it is usually the punch you don't see that knocks you out.) Also, train yourself not to instinctively blink as an attack comes towards you. The second part means that you want to know all of the possible actions that a particular limb can use, such as the lead arm coming straight, curving, upwards, etc. Both the above abilities should be developed in the process of perfecting technical and tactical actions.
2. Increase your speed of perception and reactive abilities against sudden or unforeseen variations. In the course of training, have your partner throw attacks from unusual angles, or with off-timing and work on not being "surprised" by them.

MOVEMENT TIME

Movement time can be defined as the time taken to make one simple movement, be it an offensive or defensive one.

TIMING YOUR ATTACK OR COUNTERATTACK

There are five basic times during which a hit may land against the opponent:
1. Your hit may land as the opponent is planning on preparing to move. This is known as Attack of Preparation.

2. Your hit may land when the opponent is in the midst of a movement. This is known as Attack on Development.

3. Your hit may land at the end of the opponent's attack or even as he begins to withdraw. This is known as Attack on Completion.

4. Your hit may land when the opponent's attention has been diverted or if he loses his concentration.

5. Your hit may land in the fluctuating cyclic events of tension—when the opponent tenses due to anger, etc.

LENGTHENING OPPONENT'S MOVEMENT TIME

There are several ways to cause an opponent to lose movement time.

1. By jamming him to disturb and offset his rhythm,

and

2. By using immobilization to check and control him,

and

3. By drawing a preliminary reaction in the first half of your attack.

4. By deflecting his movement and scoring—either with time hit or parry and hit, etc.

IMPROVING TIMING

The following drills are designed to help develop either one or both forms of timing. The trainer plays an extremely important role in making sure that proper distance is maintained and that the student develops good form (proper body mechanics).

1. The trainer holds both focus gloves against his chest while the student is ready in an on-guard position. (Student shouldn't be stationary, but using small footwork, body motions, etc.) The trainer then flashes a target and the student responds with the correct attack.

a. Trainer flashes backfist line.

b. Trainer flashes lead jab line.

c. Trainer flashes lead hook line.

d. Trainer flashes rear uppercut line.

e. Other hands you should practice are (see *JKD Kickboxing*):

1. The cross. 2. The body hook. 3. Then mix the various hand tools.

f. Then holding the focus gloves in the same manner work on the following kicks: 1. The front straight kick. 2. Front hook kick. 3. Rear hook (round) kick. 4. Side kick. 5. Heel hook kick. 6. Spinning kicks. 7. Mix.

g. Some of the hand combinations you can practice are:
1. Jab—cross—high lead hook.
2. Jab—cross—body hook.
3. Jab—cross—lead uppercut.
4. Jab—rear uppercut—high lead hook.
5. Jab—high lead hook—cross.
6. Jab—high lead hook—low cross.

h. Some of the foot combinations you can drill are:
1. Lead straight kick—lead hook kick—rear hook kick.
2. Lead hook kick—lead side kick.
3. Lead hook kick—spin kick.
4. Rear hook kick—heel hook kick.

i. Some hand and foot combinations you can drill are:
1. Jab—lead hook kick—cross.
2. Jab—cross—rear hook kick—or Savate chasse.
3. Step through rear hook kick—uppercut.
4. Jab—cross—rear front straight kick.
5. Lead straight kick—jab—cross.
6. Lead hook kick—cross.

Add three of your own:
7. _____
8. _____
9. _____

NOTE: In a more advanced version of this exercise, the partner can also throw punches or even kicks at the beginning, or during, or after a combination so that the student can work on defense. These drills can be done stationary or with both people moving.

2. In this drill the trainer sets a line (in this case a backfist target). The student then trains his attack against the trainer's movement. The idea is for the punch to land at precisely the moment the trainer's motion ends. Again, in the beginning stage the trainer should make sure proper distance is maintained as well as proper body mechanics used.

a. Student attacks as trainer steps forward.

b. Student attacks as trainer steps backwards.

c. Student attacks as trainer sidesteps one direction.

d. Student attacks as trainer sidesteps the other direction.

3. Using a kicking shield for the same purpose:
   a. Student times his side kick against trainer's forward step.

b. Student times his side kick against trainer's backward step.

4. Using the Thai pads for the same purpose:
Trainer holds the Thai pads in a neutral position. As he twists to his left, the student kicks the pads with a right rear leg round kick.

Remember to kick through the pad!

b. As the trainer twists to his right, the student quickly shifts his stance and fires a left round kick.

c. The trainer twists either left or right and you react with either a. or b.

5. Each partner wears a focus glove and one man initiates an attack. The idea is to intercept the opponent's attacking motion and counter with your own.

6. Moving with an opponent and attempting to score as he moves. In this case cadence and distance must be adjusted to the opponent, and the opponent is not trying to counter or offset. Several examples may be:

a. Intercepting with a straight hit.

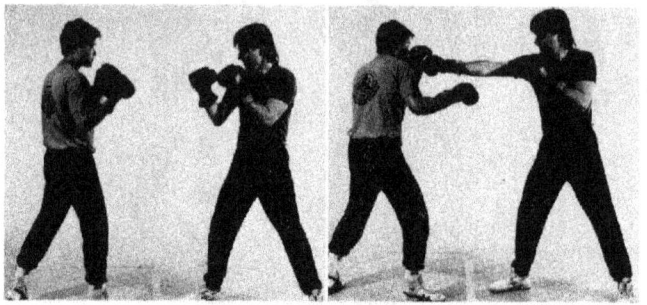

b. Intercepting with a parry and hit.

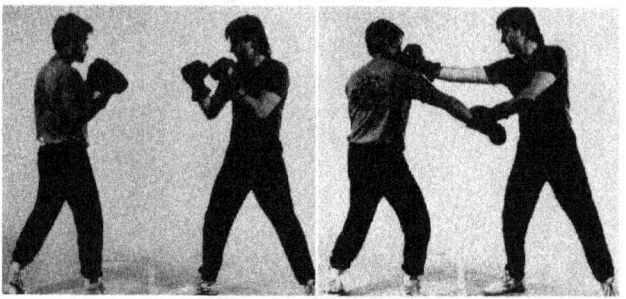

c. Body angulation with counter hit.

d. Body positioning with counter kick.

NOTE: In a more advanced version of this exercise the opponent tries to provoke errors in timing.

7. Other Timing Drills

a. Catch the punch drill—In this drill one man stands with his hands about 12 inches apart while the other man throws a controlled jab. The first man attempts to catch the punch while the second man tries to avoid being touched.

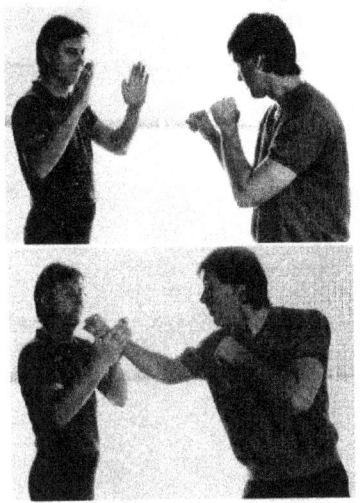

b. Pak sao drill—In this drill one man stands with his hands in prayer position while the second man is at the high reference point. As soon as the first man moves his left hand back, the second man pak saos and hits.

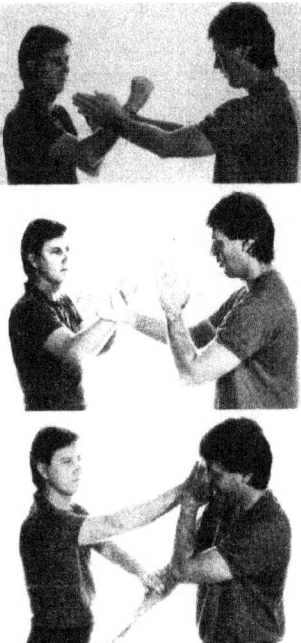

c. Swinging gate drill—In this drill you start in the high inside high reference point. As your partner attempts to slap your arm, you disengage, pak and fire a backfist.

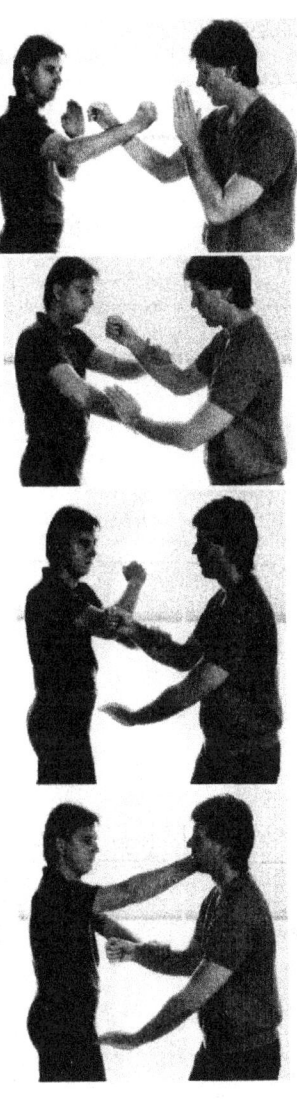

RHYTHM AND CADENCE

While rhythm can be defined as measured movement with uniform recurrence of a beat—such as 4/4 time, we are really more concerned with cadence.

Cadence in this case is the specific rhythm at which a succession of movements is executed. The speed of any particular cadence must be regulated to coincide with the opponent's. If it is too fast, the attacker will parry himself by hitting into a closed line. The attacker's cadence on his low rear cross, lead high hook was too fast and he ends up hitting into a closed line.

If it is too slow, the opponent has time to counter in the midst of the succession of movements.

By too slow a cadence the opponent has time to counter hit before the lead high hook arrives.

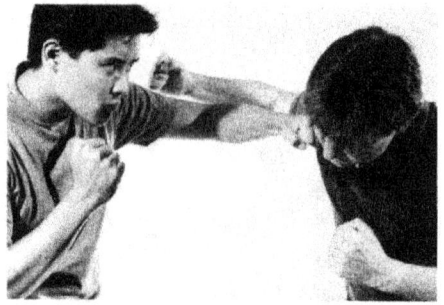

By adjusting the cadence of his attack to the opponent, the final blow lands in an open line.

The cadence of any particular sequence can be varied. For instance, we'll take the simple jab/rear cross/lead hook three punch combination. By varying the cadence we can get:

1. short—short—short
2. long—short—short
3. short—long—short
4. short—short—long
5. short—long—long
6. long—short—long
7. long—long—short
8. long—long—long

134

Training Aids for Cadence

1. Use a metronome set at various speeds and work combinations on the beat.
2. Make a cassette tape of drumbeats or tones using various cadences and work combinations on the beat.

BROKEN RHYTHM

In motion there can be established a rhythm. Natural body movement of bobbing and weaving, feinting, even punching and kicking often have a natural rhythm. In training learn to be aware of your rhythm. In drills with your training partner learn to be aware of his rhythm in both attack and defense. Once you become aware of rhythm you can work on breaking your rhythm to destroy the rhythm of your opponent's defense or to break his attacking rhythm. The breaking of any normal rhythm by a slight hesitation or an additional beat between that normal rhythm leads to broken rhythm. In other words rhythm can be broken by:

1. Motion from a slow rhythm to a fast one.
2. From fast to slow.
3. Or by pausing between two or more movements.

Broken rhythm is also referred to as "hitting on the half beat" because the motion takes place in the middle of one beat in the rhythm of an attacking sequence. Broken rhythm in both attack and counterattack is valuable because it catches the opponent when he is motor set, which makes it very difficult to counter or defend. Examples:

1. 1-2-3-4   ,   1-2-3 1/2 — 4 1/2 — 5 1/2
   Original   break   new natural rhythm
   natural
   rhythm
2. 1-2-3-4   ,   1 1/2   -2-3-4-
                   break   new natural rhythm

Breaking Your Opponent's Attacking Rhythm

Imagine the rhythm in the following jab-cross-hook combination as the defender rolls with the punches. Feel the rhythm (1-2-3) as you roll against a jab-cross-hook.

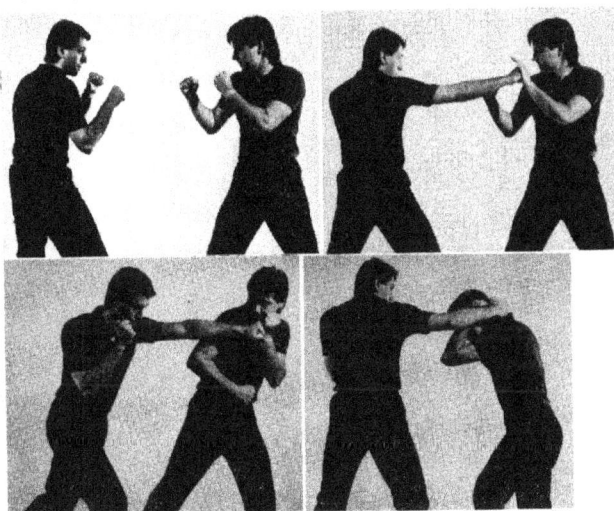

a. On the 1/2 Beat—

Here we see the rhythm of the jab-cross-hook (1-2-3) broken on the 1/2 beat. To break your opponent's rhythm on the 1/2 beat, hit him before he can complete his first movement, in this case the jab.

b. On the 1 1/2 Beat—Hit your opponent between his first and second punch.

c. On the 2 1/2 Beat—Hit your opponent between his second and third hit.

Training Aid for Broken Rhythm
Use the same metronome or cassette tapes and pick up the rhythm in your motions, then try to use a motion between two beats, on the 1/2 beat.

SECRET Jan. 2. (Tues.)

The "tool" has a double functions:—
1) to destroy anyone or anything that opposes the will of its owner
2) to sacrifice all the impulse of anger, pride, self-preservation, etc. The tool is then directed toward ourselves, a tool to kill the ego.

Personal handwritten notes by Bruce Lee.

ESSENTIAL QUALITIES

SPEED

The quality of speed can be broken down into two main categories. They are Reaction Speed and Movement Speed. Each of these main types of speed can be broken down into many minor variations such as visual awareness speed, alteration speed, footwork speed, hand trapping speed, etc. However, these are subcategories of either: 1. speed of your motor reaction; or 2. speed of your movement. It is also very diverse. A fighter may have fast hand motions but slow footwork. Likewise, another may have slower reaction speed but compensates for it with faster perceptual speed. Thus to say an individual is fast and another slow is an oversimplified generalization. A lot of one's speed is also inherent. However, various aspects of speed can be increased in everyone to some degree. Let's take a look at each type of speed in-depth.

MOVEMENT SPEED

Movement speed can be defined as the ability to generate bodily movements in the shortest possible time—be it a simple movement or a complex movement. Motor speed can be a deciding factor in one's fighting abilities.

Some of the essential prerequisites for speed are:

1. Mobility of Nervous Processes—Fine-tuned neuromuscular skills and abilities.

2. Power Performance—The ability to *explode* from one's neutral position.

3. Muscle Flexibility and Elasticity—Necessary for full range of motion and to cut down muscular resistance which can slow a movement.

4. Proper Focus of One's Attention.

5. Willpower.

Many factors other than basic speed abilities also condition movement speed. These are such things as strength, endurance, coordination, technical skill, etc.

Any punching or kicking movement is basically a ballistic motion (like a bullet). On the way to its target the weapon is being acted on by inertia. Even as your arm or leg is extending on its way outward the antagonistic muscles are preparing to fire and slow the movement or stop it in order to prevent you from injuring yourself. If it doesn't then you may end up hyperextending the joint. Even so you must keep the antagonistic muscles as relaxed as possible to truly "explode" a punch. In this case, the more powerful the explosion of your initial movement is, the faster the punch or kick will travel.

REACTION SPEED

Reaction speed, like movement speed, is also conditioned by other factors. These include: proper focus and concentration on the object to be responded to; fatigue (physical or mental); awareness (visual, aural, tactile), etc. It can also be divided into: 1. simple motor reactions; and 2. complex motor reactions. A simple reaction may be all that is required against a single attacking motion, whereas a complex one may be necessary against a combination attacking motion.

Most of the reactions prevalent in martial arts are complex in that, due to constant and sudden changes in situations or actions, the martial artist has to select from several possible actions the one adequate to the situation.

SPEED IMPROVEMENT

Basically there are two ways to improve one's speed. These are:

1. Increase the positive factors—improve strength, power, endurance, awareness, etc.

2. Decrease the negative aspects—improve neuromuscular coordination (skill), improve flexibility, etc.

The basis for improving speed is to include a strictly regulated session devoted to instilling movement speed or developing reaction speed in your training program. And during the workout the martial artist must attempt to reach his highest speed or surpass it by the highest possible neuromuscular coordination which corresponds to the physical action being trained. The technique which is being trained must also have been mastered and stabilized at medium speeds first to ensure proper body mechanics.

The four basic considerations to be included in a speed training workout are:

1. Amount of Work—The amount of work at maximum speed which best develops speed is relatively small per session due to the high demands on the neuromuscular system.

2. Intervals—The rest intervals between repetitions should ensure an optimum recovery level of the performance level.

3. Psychology—High demands should be placed on the martial artist in the session to induce a strong application of willpower.

4. Safety—Full fitness should be ensured before training sessions are used to isolate and develop speed, as such work

places high demands on the muscles, tendons and ligaments. A careful warm-up including stretching and relaxation exercises is therefore a must, and training should be stopped in the event of muscle pains or cramps. Physical freshness is also necessary, and speed work should not be done following tiring activities.

MOVEMENT SPEED IMPROVEMENT METHOD

The recurrent execution of a particular action aiming at the maximum movement speed. Any of the timing devices on the market today have great merit as they help to develop movement as well as reaction speed.

Simple Reaction Speed Improvement—A recurrent reaction by the action to the suddenly appearing (predesigned) motion with the objective being to reduce the time taken to react. This can be practiced both isolated (with trainer and student stationary) or with the student having to move with and relate to a moving opponent (trainer).

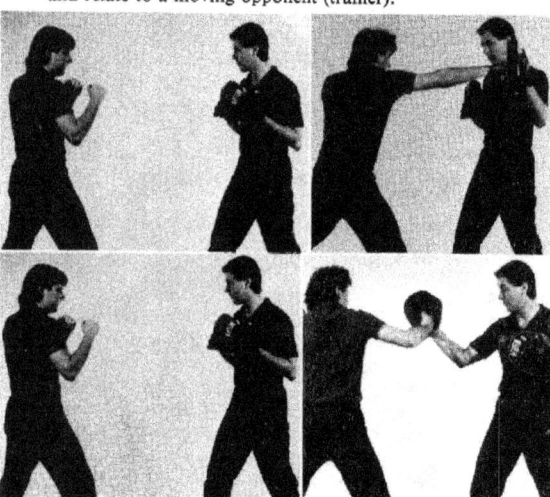

Complex Reaction Speed Improvement—The main way is the modeling in the course of training of integral situations in which the student must select the appropriate response. Gradually increasing the number of variants in action allowed to one training partner in a definite order together with the number of response actions allowed to the other partner. Light sparring is also helpful.

TRAINING METHODS TO INCREASE SPEED ASPECTS

1. Reducing the spatial limits in which action takes place (sparring in a smaller ring).
2. Reducing the time limit allowed to execute actions (shortening the time of a sparring bout, or the time it takes to complete a combination).
3. Using boxing gloves/wearing shoes of various weight (heavier, standard, lighter) when sparring.
4. Shadow boxing with weights. These must be small, five ounces to possibly one pound. The more weight you use the more your neuromuscular system will change and affect the "grooving" of the motion.
5. Increasing body weight through the use of weight vests, etc., that will not hamper proper body movements. Again the amount of weight must not be too high. In no way do we recommend "air" kicking with weights around the ankles.

DRILLS TO IMPROVE REACTION TIME

1. All types of sparring (see Chapter 10).
2. Kali stick training.
3. Kali dagger training.
4. Television drill. Watch any filmed TV show. Punch or kick whenever the film cuts to another shot.
5. Stand facing a wall, about 10 to 12 feet from it, and have someone throw a tennis ball over your head at the wall. Try to catch the ball as it bounces off the wall. Move closer to have the ball thrown harder as you get faster. This exercise improves overall reaction time. For coordination do the above drill while standing on one leg. If you don't have a partner, then you can throw the ball yourself making sure that it comes back at various angles.
6. In an on-guard position throw up a hacky sack as you return your front hand to its original on-guard position and catch it as if you were punching. Do this with a jab.

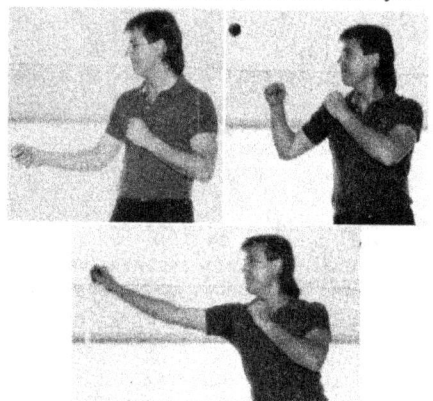

Do it also with a cross, hook and uppercut.

POWER

Power is the ability to exert strength quickly. In fact, in Europe it is often referred to as speed-strength. The primary key is to develop the greatest amount of force in the shortest amount of time. The initial concentric contraction of the prime mover is literally an "explosion" within the muscle and incorporation of all the body parts to impact maximum torque (proper body mechanics).

In this example of a hook punch, the lower body is not being used, resulting in a loss of power.

Here the entire body is being put behind the punch, starting from the foot, through the knee, hip, waist, shoulder, elbow and finally the fist. This is an example of expressing power using a stationary base.

When a blow lands we want the entire body behind it to maximize the power; thus the term "hitting with the whole body" and not merely the arm or leg. Russian studies have proven that approximately one third of the power in a punch comes from the feet and lower body, one third comes from the waist, and one third comes from the shoulder and arm.

To express power while moving forward we need to make sure that the punch lands just a fraction of a second before our lead foot touches the ground, allowing the person's total weight to be projected into the opponent instead of downward into the floor.

TRAINING AIDS FOR POWER

The primary ways to increase power are:
1. Increase your speed, strength remaining constant.
2. Increase your strength, speed remaining constant.
3. Increase both speed and strength.

Both speed and strength can be increased by the use of such plyometric exercises as follows:

1. Depth jumping and various forms of jumping for leg explosiveness.

2. Explosive pushups for arm power.

3. Lying on back and returning medicine ball after it's dropped.

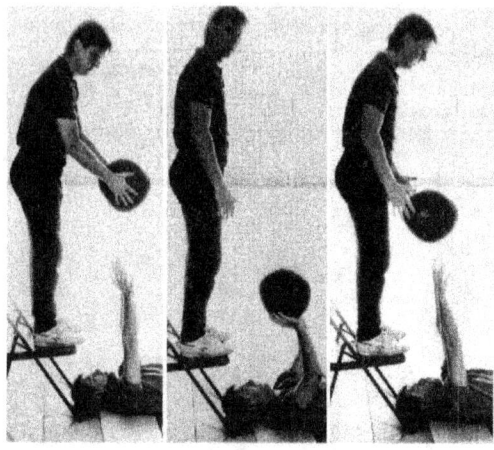

For a thorough breakdown of plyometrics we suggest you read *Plyometrics* by Michael Yessis and Frederick Hatfield.

Another excellent method to gain power is the use of a weapon to develop torque. This is similar to why boxers used to chop down trees with an axe to develop body motion.

Finally we recommend weight training. While weight training will develop strength, for power you need to concentrate on exercises that require speed to perform such as the clean and jerk.

ENDURANCE

Endurance can be defined as the capacity to resist fatigue. High levels of endurance facilitate the mastery of a lot of hard work during training and allow high quality movements and perfect solutions to both technical and tactical problems for the entire training session. There is an old saying that "When endurance goes out the window everything else usually follows." Well-developed endurance abilities are also important for a quick recovery following a hard workout.

There are various types of endurance as well, such as strength-endurance and speed-endurance, basic endurance and specific endurance. In training, the so-called basic endurance is the functional base for all the other various kinds of endurance. It is during this basic endurance training that one's personality traits such as self-discipline and willpower are developed. Motivation and willingness to take pain are two psychological elements involved in such training.

ENDURANCE IMPROVEMENT—Endurance training must be considered in light of the actual requirement of what you want to achieve. There are three primary methods which can be used to improve one's endurance. These are:

1. Increase the duration of the training exercise or session.
2. Increase the speed used during training exercise or session.
3. Decrease the rest intervals used during training exercises in the session.

EXAMPLE—By varying the work/rest intervals of a 30-minute heavy bag workout, you can develop different levels of endurance. For example, using a heavy bag you might choose to work it:

1. 30 minutes constantly (no rest—medium pace).
2. Three-minute rounds with one minute rest between rounds.

3. One-minute rounds—one-minute rest in between.
4. 30-second rounds—30-second rest in between.

The lower the time of the round, the higher the intensity of the work should be.

COORDINATION

Coordination is the quality which enables the martial artist to integrate all the powers and capacities he has into the effective doing of an act. It is the ability to move and organize yourself around your own physical body. Coordinative abilities differ from technical skills in that they exist as prerequisites for subsequent motor actions.

Seven coordinative abilities can be differentiated by their characteristics, and while all seven are fundamental to martial arts as a whole they may appear in quite different values in each person.

These abilities are:

1. Combinatory Ability—The ability to coordinate parts of body movements and single movements with one another in relation to a total movement of the body towards a given action. In contests between individuals where there is confrontation with a moving opponent, numerous complicated and rapid adjustments are necessary (combining lower body action with upper body action against a constantly shifting opponent).

2. Orientation—Knowing where you are at any given moment. It is the ability to analyze and change the position and movement of the body in space and at the same time relate to the area in which the action is taking place (a boxing ring, for instance).

3. Differential Ability—The ability to achieve a high degree of accuracy and fine adjustment of separate body movements and mechanical phases of a total body movement. This is related to the perfecting and stabilizing of technical skills and their actual application in bouts between individuals where there is a high precision in various situations despite the actions of opponents.

3a. *Agility* would be included in this category. Agility is the ability to exercise a fine coordination of the movements of the various parts of the body as well as the ability to relax the muscles which produces a conscious tuning of the muscle tone. (See relaxation exercises at the end of this chapter.)

4. Balance—The ability to maintain the whole body in dynamic equilibrium.

5. Reactive Ability (Good Reactions)—The ability to initiate quickly and to perform rapid and well-directed actions following a signal.

6. Adaptive Ability—The ability to modify a sequence of actions to new conditions, or observing anticipated changes in the situation, or to continue the sequence in another way.

7. Rhythmic Sense—The ability to observe the characteristic uniform recurrence of a beat within measured movement.

In the book *Fundamentals of Sports Training*, Matveyev states that "In mastering a new exercise, an athlete not only qualitatively replenishes his motor experience but 'trains his training level,' as an ability to learn new forms of coordinating movements."

COORDINATION IMPROVEMENT METHODS

1. Vary the execution of the movement—Separate phases or partial movements of the body are modified. Examples are:

   a. Performing a punching sequence such as a jab/cross/lead hook in reverse order (hook/cross/jab).

   b. "Mirror" execution—working in opposite lead from which you are accustomed to.

2. Make changes in external conditions. Examples are:

   a. Reducing or enlarging the sparring area.

   b. Varying glove weight.

   c. Change in partners once or several times during a training exercise.

   d. Change the surface conditions upon which you are training—sand, gravel, on the side of a hill, slick surface, etc.

   e. Varying the lighting—very bright, dark, moonlight, etc.

3. Combining increasingly difficult mechanical skills. This requires that the individual actions have been mastered in detail, as otherwise too many faults can appear or unplausible combinations attempted.

4. Actions under Time Pressure—An exercise that has been completely mastered should be performed as quickly as possible following a given signal to develop reactions while at the same time maintaining good form and motions that are as perfect as possible.

5. Vary the Information Sources Available:

   a. Performing actions while blindfolded.

   b. Removing hearing abilities.

6. Actions Following Disorientation—A complex movement practiced after being turned around several times or after several forward or backward rolls.

7. Other Aids to Coordination:

   a. Juggling

   b. Dance classes—ballet, tap, etc.

   c. Tai Chi

   d. Gymnastics

   e. Playing hacky sack

Notice that many of these aids and ideas are outside of most martial arts training. For growth, don't be bound and stay just within the confines of your style or even martial arts. You can go outside of martial arts to help your martial art.

PRECISION

Precision can be defined as accuracy in a particular movement or projection of force. It means being able to place your weapon of attack exactly on the desired location. It is one thing to have the ability to hit a stationary target precisely, but much more difficult to place that hit perfectly on a target that is not only moving but also trying to score on you.

As it is a fine skill, precision work should be practiced when you are freshest for the maximum benefit. It can be trained simultaneously with speed work, for it is better to concentrate on speed and accuracy first before working the same action with speed and power.

PRECISION IMPROVEMENT

1. Moving with partner and hitting/kicking focus gloves at various positions while glove is still moving and not set in static position.

2. Trainer holds focus glove so that if hit or kick is not dead center of glove his hand wobbles or pivots.

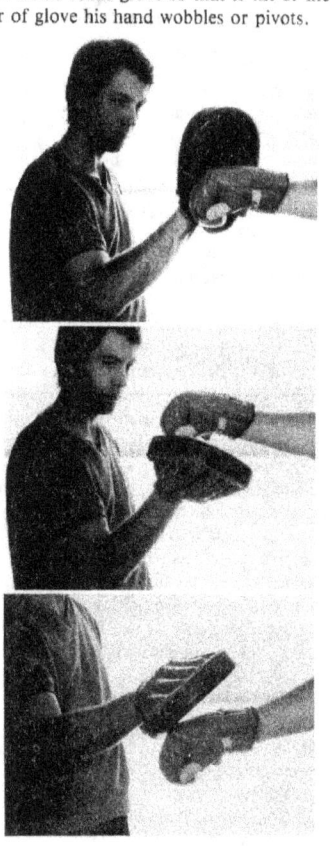

3. Use of Impax focus glove which must be hit dead center to register maximum power.

4. Training with smaller targets such as bag gloves, smaller pads, or hitting designated small targets on kicking shield, heavy bag.

5. The use of the top and bottom bag for kicking as well as punching.

6. Savate training method of placing glove as target.

142

For example, using body tilt to facilitate faster sidestep.

7. Hand/eye coordination exercises or games—handball, darts, etc.

8. Imagine an egg in your heavy bag. Try to just crack the shell of the imaginary egg with a kick. Then smash it.

BALANCE

Balance is the quality of achieving an inner relationship between all the points of your body. It is an active state, constantly going on and continually shifting. Thus the balance you seek is dynamic balance, or balance in motion, not in stillness (stances). Sometimes it is even possible to use a momentary loss of balance to facilitate faster movement.

BALANCE IMPROVEMENT

The following exercises can help improve your awareness of your balance.

1. Stand on one leg, then close your eyes and try to maintain as still a position as possible.

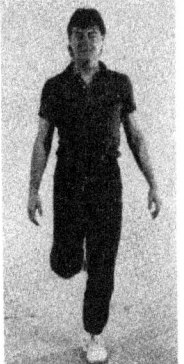

143

2. While standing on one leg, shift your body into various angles and positions and try to find the balance point on each one.

3. Walking across a balance beam placed several inches off the ground, keep your eyes focused on a ball which is hanging by a string and swinging back and forth at the opposite end of the beam.

BODY FEEL AND GOOD FORM

Body feel and good form are combined here because they both relate closely to the quality of one's movements. The adherence to certain movement parameters decides the effectiveness of any motion. What this basically means is that there is a best way to do any motion. Ascertaining the optimum movement parameters of a given motion and aiming for their use in training increases the chance of success.

The basic principles of efficient motion are:

1. Improve the physical skills involved first.

   a. Eliminate any unnecessary movement. From a neutral on-guard position the attacker fires a lead jab without any unnecessary movement.

As you can see from the sequence, by pulling his arm back prior to punching, the attacker telegraphs his intention.

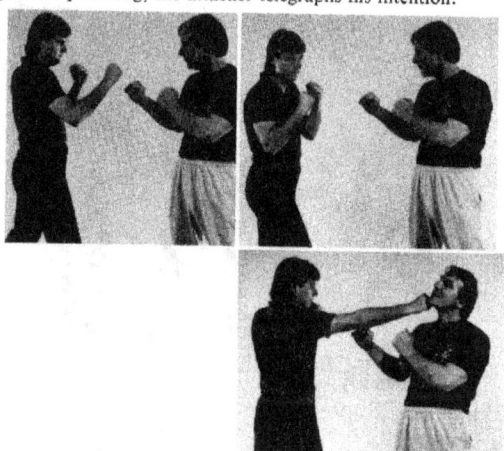

   b. Eliminate unnecessary muscle activity—within even the necessary movement by maintaining relaxation in the muscles antagonistic to the movement and even keep the muscles responsible for the movement relaxed.

   c. All movements should be made in the correct direction. For example, proper body alignment and line of direction of force in a hook.

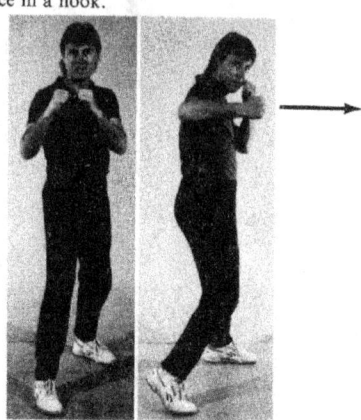

2. Improve your physical condition so that a given level of work requires less energy from anaerobic sources. (Keep a good level of physical fitness.)

TRAINING AIDS FOR BODY FEEL AND GOOD FORM

1. The way in which you perform a motion in training is the way you will perform the same action in a combative situation. This is due to the fact that you have "grooved" that action into your neuromuscular system, and in a pressure situation your body will literally "switch to automatic pilot." So if you train your recovery after a kick sloppily, you will do that in a fight.

Sloppy recovery after a side kick.

2. Utilize the "whole-part-whole" training method. You start by practicing the whole motion. Then you can break it down into its component parts such as: a. initiation; b. landing; and c. recovery. Then always return back to the whole motion.

3. Do as many of the techniques as possible in front of a mirror and look for the following:
    a. That you keep a well-covered position during any strike.
    b. That you hit and return on the same line.
    c. That you avoid any unnecessary preparation prior to your attack (drawing back, unnecessary footwork, facial expression that might give you away, etc.).

4. Use of a swimming pool. The water adds resistance to your motion and allows you to feel the direction of your force and improve strength. After training a motion in the water, get out and practice the same thing on dry land.

AWARENESS

There are three types of awareness—visual, audio, and tactile. Tactile is also known as sensitivity and was covered in an earlier chapter, so we will concentrate here on visual and audio.

Awareness allows us to be consciously informed of an opponent's action, impending action or reaction. And the better informed we are about our opponent's actions the better we are equipped to deal with that person. That fraction of time or slight edge we gain by increased awareness can make the difference between success and defeat.

Audio and visual awareness training is an important part of the Jun Fan training curriculum from the first stages of training. And such training drills should be maintained even in advanced martial artists. Lee himself stated, "As I get older my speed may decrease, but my awareness will increase."

Good recovery after a side kick.

Prerequisites for increased awareness are a relaxed and yet alert mental attitude and proper focus of attention. The following awareness drills have been an integral part of the Jun Fan curriculum since the late 1960s.

Visual Stimuli—This is more important for combat as most of your cues to action will be visual in nature.
  1. Using a flashlight and shining it against a wall.
      a. Stationary flashlight—When it moves, you move.
      b. Moving flashlight—When it stops, you move.
  2. Punch or kick at any change of body position to the trainer.

  3. Punch or kick at any minor move of the trainer—no matter how slight.

  4. Holding a closed fist up, then opening it suddenly and unrhythmically.

Audio Stimuli—
  1. Voice command to initiate a strike.
  2. Use of clackers, or drums, or piano to initiate a strike.

OTHER AIDS
  1. The "OOH" drill—This drill can be practiced either in a stationary relaxed or on-guard position, or while moving with footwork in on-guard position. As soon as the student is aware of the stimulus (visual or audio) he responds to it by shouting "OOH." The emphasis is to cut down the time between stimulus and response.
      1a. The same as above, but instead of shouting you respond with a designated punch or kick.

  2. Heavy bag drill—One student moves around the heavy bag in an on-guard position while the partner holds the heavy bag from behind. As soon as the partner removes a hand away from the bag or lifts a leg, the student responds with a kick or punch.

3. Focus glove drill—Partner moves the glove all around in circular motions. The moment he stops a glove you hit or kick it.

4. Partner has three tennis balls, each a different color. He calls out a sequence such as green, yellow, orange, then tosses the balls at you. You respond by hitting the balls in the sequence he called out.

TRAINING PERIPHERAL VISION

1. The student focuses on the finger of one of the trainer's hands which is pointing at him. The trainer then moves his other hand from the outside in until it is visible at the very outside of the student's vision. While keeping his eyes on the finger pointing at him, the student must try to pick up the letters being drawn with the other hand by the trainer.

2. The student stands in an on-guard position or a natural stance while two other students stand on each side of him just on the edge of his peripheral vision. They take turns striking at him and he counters.

RELAXATION AND VISUALIZATION

Relaxation is one of the most important qualities. Both mental and physical relaxation are necessary for efficient learning of new tasks. If you are not mentally relaxed you will be too tense and nervous to really concentrate on learning a new skill or to be able to focus on your opponent. Bruce Lee said that in combat you should have an "everyday mind," that is, a mind uncluttered with fear or anger. In combat you should be mentally relaxed. Then you can fire a punch or a kick with emotional content. To be able to turn your adrenaline off and on as if you were turning on and off a light, he said, was the essence of a skilled combative mind. Many times an inexperienced fighter will be so nervous in the dressing room before a fight that he will have little left when he gets into the ring. He has in a real sense used up his adrenaline before he needed to use it. As the fighter becomes more experienced, he learns to control his emotions.

If you are attacked in the street, you will not have the time to use up your adrenaline. Your problem will be to control it. You will need to try and stay both mentally and physically relaxed which is the essence of the "everyday mind." When you hit you need a strong enough image of something you hate so much that your adrenaline instantly fires giving great power to your strike. But you must practice this so it is controlled anger (emotional content) which can be turned off as easily as it is turned on. For each student this mental training is as important as the physical training. Since each individual is different no one can give you the proper mental attitude. You may be quite successful sparring in the gym, but under the pressure of a real fight your training can go out the window in a burst of uncontrolled anger. In that case you may find yourself slugging wildly.

No one can teach you this combative mind, only experience can. But it is possible to work on it in the gym. For example, when you punch a heavy bag or kick the Thai pads try to do it with emotional content. This should be done after you've acquired the skill, not as you are learning it.

Mental training begins with relaxation exercises. The following exercises should be done at least 20 minutes a day until you can instantly relax anytime you need to. Mental and physical relaxation go hand in hand. If you are physically relaxed your mind will be also and vice versa. Tape the following two exercises until you can learn them by heart. Do them before you train.

1. Progressive Muscle Relaxation—This exercise takes practice but is quite easy once you get the hang of it. The idea is to first tense a muscle group so you will have an awareness of how muscle tension works. Then you relax the muscles to feel the release of tension. You should do this exercise in a quiet room, stretched out on your back on a comfortable mat or rug. Breathe in deeply. Then exhale slowly, feeling the relaxation of tension as you do so. Tense each major muscle group, then release the tension. Inhale as you tense, exhale as you relax. If you do this exercise faithfully, you will be able to relax your muscles without tensing them first.

1. Flex your feet up toward your head. Relax.
2. Press your feet downward, tensing your calves. Relax.
3. Tighten your thighs and buttocks, pressing them to the floor. Relax.
4. Arch your back upward. Relax.
5. Tighten your stomach muscles. Relax.
6. Breathe in deeply. Exhale slowly and relax.
7. Shrug your shoulders. Relax.
8. Clench your fists. Relax.
9. Bend your elbows up to tense your biceps. Relax.
10. Press your arms down to tense your biceps and forearms. Relax.
11. Flex your neck. Relax.
12. Clench your jaw and lips. Relax.
13. Close your eyes tightly and frown. Relax.
14. Wrinkle your forehead. Relax.

2. Breath Relaxation—On your tape for this exercise make sure you leave enough time to relax each part of your body before you move on. Lie on your back with your hands at your sides, palms down, and your feet flat on the floor. When you are comfortable, breathe and concentrate on the image of riding your breath. "Watch with your mind your breath go way out. . . . Like a switchboard start to unplug your impulses. . . . Breathe into what is tense and tension will go out with your breath . . . relax . . . no tension . . . ride your breath . . . relax your eyes . . . mouth . . . jaw. . . . Let your tension out of your body with your breath as you ride it . . . sink into the floor. . . . Relax your neck . . . shoulders . . . float into the ground. . . . Relax your arms . . . hands . . . fingers . . . torso . . . ride your breath. . . . Relax your thighs . . . tops of legs . . . calves . . . feet . . . toes . . . continue to ride your breath. . . . You're now totally relaxed and floating. Let your thoughts happen. Don't pursue them."

VISUALIZATION

Once you are totally relaxed you can move on to visualization which is to mentally rehearse a technique or skill. This mental rehearsal is done by most world class athletes. For example, Dwight Stones, before he would high jump, saw himself clearing the bar with perfect form. It's really easy to do and quite valuable. For example, with your mind imagine you are kicking the heavy bag with perfect form and explosive power. Mentally rehearse this kick for at least five minutes. Then get up and kick the bag. Try it, and see what happens. We're sure you will be satisfied with the result.

SECRET

When there is a particle of dust in your eye, the world becomes a narrow path. — Have your mind completely free from objects — and how much this life expands.

SATORI — the awakening from a dream. Awakening and self-realization and seeing into one's own being — these are synonymous.

Personal handwritten notes by Bruce Lee.

TACTICS AND STRATEGY

An old fencing proverb states that "to hit a worthy opponent with a complex movement is satisfying and shows one's mastery of technique; to hit the same opponent by a simple movement is a sign of greatness." It is fine to be able to go out and defeat an opponent with simple moves, but sometimes you may have to push it to the very edge and use every means at your disposal. Those means are tactics. Tactics allow you to utilize your capacities economically and to their maximum.

Tactical actions only become visible with physical actions. A physical solution is a complex activity composed equally of mental as well as physical abilities and skills. It is the result of productive and creative thought connected with an optimum use of physical capacities, technical skill, and mental qualities as well as the product of observation and analysis of a combative situation.

The decision to use any particular method of attack or attacking action is greatly influenced and in some ways even decided by the opponent. His physical size, mental attitude, method of fighting and technical skills all play integral parts in the situation. This is what Bruce Lee meant by "You are my technique. Your technique decides my technique."

Any tactical problem is first solved mentally and then physically. The mind's job is to find the best solution for the tactical task at hand in the shortest possible time on the basis of knowledge of one's own capacities and analysis of the situation. The fighter must be sure of his knowledge, physical skills and abilities, confident in his decision, and convinced that these things are sufficient to translate his tactical solution into reality.

The prime prerequisite for high-level tactical training is that the martial artist must have complete command of his weapons systems (arms/legs, etc.) and their variants. Only when you don't have to *consciously* be concerned with such things as balance, freedom of movement, attacking and defensive motions can you then concentrate on the more tactical elements. Think of anything you learned; riding a bicycle, for example. Remember when you first started how it seemed like so much to try and do at one time—pedaling, steering, balancing and braking. But as you became more proficient these actions became almost unconscious and you were then free to look at all the things around you as you were riding. It is the same in martial arts.

While it is true that no opponent should be attacked unwisely without first having ascertained their reactions with probing attacks and feints, sometimes this is not possible. One may not have the time to decide, or one's choices may be limited due to extraneous circumstances. In this case, the better trained you are the higher your chances of success. Likewise, the wider the variety of attacks, counterattacks, fighting methods (Muay Thai, Savate, Karate, etc.) that you have been exposed to in training, the less chance you stand of being surprised by unfamiliar motions.

The Mental and Physical Process of a Tactical Action

1. Perception and analysis of the situation.
2. Consideration of the solution of the specific tactical task.
3. Physical execution of the tactical action.

Guidelines for Tactical Training

A. Train your powers of observation and analytical skills. Boxers watch films of other boxers, football teams watch videotapes of other teams. Observe other fighting methods and even other students you train with; seek out and mentally record any idiosyncracies. Analyze and "tune" yourself up to what actions and counteractions can be used to defeat them. Don't waste time with idle gossip between sparring bouts—observe and be aware.

B. Develop and maintain a high level of technical skills, physical capacities, and mental abilities.

C. Organize your training program to include tactical training as an important part of the overall training process.

Basic Tactics

1. Use your head, fight with your head. Out-think the opponent and you can out-hit him.
2. Have a firm command of your technical skills and physical abilities.
3. Stay loose and relaxed.
4. Confident plus at all times. If you're hurt or tired, try not to show it.
5. Keep moving—well-balanced and economical motions.
6. Maintain a well-covered, balanced ready position.

7. As soon as the opponent comes into range—HIT!

8. Puzzle and confuse the opponent—constant variety in attack and defense. Never do the same thing twice in succession.

9. Do exactly what the opponent doesn't want or expect you to do.

10. Whenever the opponent gets set to hit or kick—MOVE!

11. Mean business when you hit, and hit confidently, not half-heartedly or timidly.

12. Maintain proper focus of attention—a "careful watchfulness" of opponent and his actions.

13. Never underestimate any opponent at any time.

Types of Adversaries

There are many types of opponents, but they can usually be categorized into four basic types:
1. Those that give ground.
2. Those that parry.
3. Those that stop-hit.
4. Those that seek to attack.

The following are some of the main tactical actions that can best be utilized against each type of opponent:
1. Those that give ground:
   a. Sudden change of rhythm, uncrispy entrance.
   b. Preparation (line close) hand immobilization attack, occasionally followed by progressive indirect attack or single angulated attack.
2. Those that parry:
   a. Progressive indirect attack.
   b. False attack then—
      1. Timed stroke.
      2. Hand immobilization attack.
      3. Close-range tactics.
3. Those that stop-hit:
   a. Use of counter-time.
   b. Shift to grappling.
4. Those who attack:
   a. Stop-hit or counter-time.
   b. Hand immobilization attack.
   c. Shift into grappling.

Tactics Against Various Types of Fighters
1. *Tall Opponent*
   a. Sidestep and counter.
   b. Fast in and out movement combined with attack to face.
3. *Long-range Fighter*
   a. Force continually.
   b. Close to short range.
   c. Counter to body.
4. *Slugger*
   a. Constant movement to not allow opponent to get set.
   b. Attack suddenly and shift out immediately.
5. *Counter-Fighter*
   a. Try to draw the attack.
   b. Carry attack but be ready to counter-time.
   c. Constant aggressive action to keep opponent off-balance.
6. *Rusher*
   a. Sidestep or angle off and counter.
   b. Dissolve or bounce attack away.

Fighting an Opponent in Unmatched Lead

There are certain adjustments in your on-guard position that prove to be useful if the opponent you're fighting is opposite to your own (left lead vs. right lead). These shifts are:

1. Carry your lead hand slightly higher than usual to offset your opponent's lead hand, and try to keep your lead foot slightly outside of the opponent's. This position helps nullify the opponent's lead hook punch and puts you in position to bridge on the outside.

2. Use footwork and body angulation to aid in zoning away from the opponent's rear arm and leg.

3. Observe whether your opponent is in a closed-guard or open-guard position and observe the targets that are open to attack either inside or outside.

Concealing Kicking Intentions

To utilize a kicking attack without first distracting or offsetting the opponent invites a good possibility that the opponent can counter your action. To reduce the chances of such a counter, certain methods of distraction can be used. These distractions can be: (a) visual; (b) auditory; or (c) combined. Some examples of the various types of distractions are shown below. The motions have been exaggerated for viewer clarity.

1. Toss finger jab towards opponent's face.

2. Finger flick, finger fan to cover in between kicks being used in combination.

3. One hand extends, one hand slaps thigh.

4. Clapping hands together.

5. Extending rear hand outward, upward, downward, etc.

6. Extending lead hand upward and forward.

7. Quickly glancing downward, up, left, right.

8. Sink body low then kick high.

9. Raise body high then kick low.

The use of the finger flick, finger fan motions are generally used as distractions between kicks being thrown in combination in order to help offset the possibility of the opponent's countering you while in the midst of your attack.

In-fighting Tactics

Various types of close quarter attacks can be used not only to score a hit while in tight, but also to offset the opponent's balance and prevent counterattacks. In-fighting motions include:

1. Shoving the opponent's lead or rear shoulder.

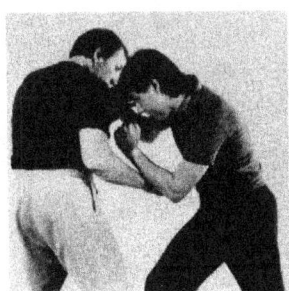 

2. Shoving the opponent's lead or rear hip.

3. Punching into opponent's lead or rear shoulder.

4. Butting into opponent with shoulder.

5. Slamming shoulder upward into opponent's jaw.

6. Buckling opponent's knee (with or without hit).

7. Spinning or twisting the opponent off-balance.

8. Shoving the opponent away.

9. The use of close-quarter pinching, hair pulling, stomping, etc.

Crispy Versus Uncrispy Motions

The term "crispy" means that a motion, be it single or in combination, is thrown sharply and tidily. "Uncrispy" on the other hand means untidily, and is sometimes referred to as "throwing garbage." Each type of motion can be used successfully to offset the other.

TRAINING METHODOLOGY

The Art is both a "Science and an "Art"
Knowledge of the art is the "Science"
Doing of the art is the "Art"

OVERALL STRUCTURE

Training is the entire process of preparation of a martial artist for the highest levels of performance. It comprises all the learning processes and elements, including self-teaching by the martial artist, which are aimed at improving one's overall abilities. Therefore, the training process should be organized with a lot of foresight. The better the process you use, the better the results you should achieve. Planning calls for the creative work of the instructor based on comprehensive knowledge and training methods. The trainer must consider in a creative manner the connection between the organization of training and the development of personality and performance.

Lack of understanding as to how the various elements in Jun Fan are bound up into a single 'whole' makes it impossible to understand the essence of the training process and to master the methods of its practical structuring and planning. It then dissolves into a haphazard accumulation of various pieces of a puzzle without any idea as to what the finished picture will look like. Without this correlation of elements, the various components of Jun Fan such as punching, kicking, trapping, and grappling will sit as separate links and look like this:

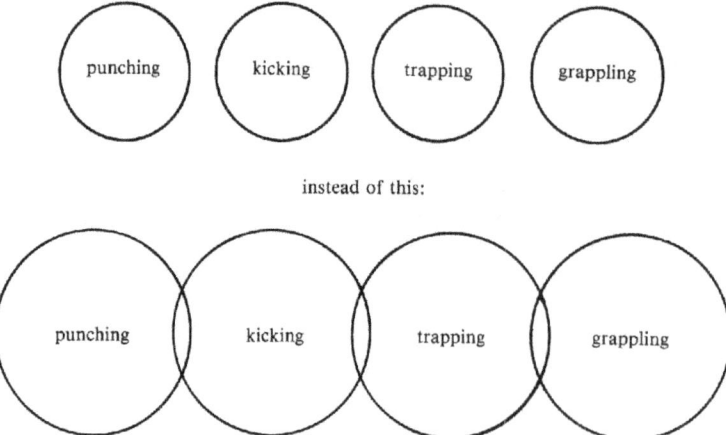

instead of this:

The main tasks, which should be seen and tackled as a whole during a martial artist's training, are:

1. Developing Personality—Developing positive attitudes, good habits, self-discipline.
2. Conditioning—Development of stamina, power, speed. Building essential prerequisites of high efficiency.
3. Technique and Coordination Training—Enables the martial artist to make economical and optimum use of his physical condition.
4. Tactical Training—Enables a martial artist to make optimum use of his physical condition and psychological capacity, in responding effectively to an opponent's strengths and weaknesses and in adapting to any situation.
5. Mental Training—Development of the martial artist's intellectual faculties, improvement of training knowledge and principles, and the ability to creatively apply such knowledge to training.

Periodization of Training

When you look at the various technical components which are integral in Jun Fan such as Western boxing, kickboxing, hand trapping, grappling, etc., you may wonder how to fit all the various facets into any sort of cohesive training program that assures continual growth. Integrating the components is achieved by using a training principle which in athletics is referred to as 'periodization in training'. Periodization is described as the continuous sequence of periodic cycles or phases in the process of building up a standard of performance. With so many different functions (speed, endurance, power, technique, etc.) it becomes practical, and sometimes necessary, to concentrate on some of these functions at certain periods.

In periodization the training year is broken down into several major periods, each several months long. These are then broken down into smaller phases of anywhere between one to several weeks. These can then again be broken down into weekly and even daily cycles. These small cycles serve as building blocks from which the average training cycles are built. Each is connected with the previous and following one. The phases or cycles apply to each various aspect, such as boxing, and follow a pattern from general to specific. Let's look at an example of how a single year might be broken down into three phases of training:

PHASE I

This phase would consist of general conditioning, cardiovascular training, muscle strength training, combined with improving the functional level of individual performance factors (basic weapon development, footwork and mobility, etc.). This phase is of paramount importance as it sets the base for all future work, both general and specific. Inadequate preparation at this stage is a prescription for future problems.

PHASE II

Involves transforming the performance factors which have been developed in the previous phase into new higher and more complex standards of performance. Combative attitude and technical problems are stressed while maintaining the level of physical condition achieved in the prior phase.

PHASE III

This phase is concerned with the elimination of known weaknesses, correction of faults, stabilization of the newly acquired skills and abilities, and the engagement in sparring. How long each phase should be depends on how many technical or tactical skills and techniques have to be learned, and the level of the student. Training is, to a great extent, an individual matter. Performance is the sum of numerous factors, which can vary from individual to individual, even if ultimately the same results are achieved. A martial artist deficient in power may compensate for it by superior technique; inferior technique may be compensated for by aggressiveness. For this reason it is very important to identify and fully mobilize each individual's potentials.

To be on the alert mean to be deadly serious, to be deadly serious mean to be sincere to oneself, and it is sincerity that finally lead one to discover the Way.

Personal handwritten notes by Bruce Lee.

Individual Training Sessions

The entire training process is comprised of a multitude of separate training sessions. The structure of a separate training session should be such that it is an integral link in the total training chain, and aimed at achieving a maximum training effect in the particular aspect(s) being worked on in that session.

The breakdown of a typical training session might look like:

A. Loosening Up—Getting rid of any muscular tension, attuning to purpose of the lessons, etc.

B. Warming Up—

    1. General—Increase cardiac output, mobilize circulatory system, increase lung ventilation and raise body temperature. Mainly simple and familiar exercises to keep the student moving without interruption—jogging, skipping rope, cycling. The intensity is gradually increased.

    2. Specialized—Here the martial artist prepares for the main phase by getting accustomed to certain movements he will use (shadow boxing, shadow kickboxing, etc.).

C. Main Phase—Training to help promote the development of or consolidate the martial artist's level of performance. It is broken into two sections:

    1. Technical training, the process of learning or perfecting technical elements. This demands utmost concentration and that is possible only if the martial artist is fresh and in an optimum ready state. Speed and power should be developed in this half, perhaps in conjunction with technical skills.

    2. Basic endurance development—such as circuit training on equipment like heavy bag, speed bag, focus gloves, etc.

D. Final Phase—Recovery phase. Relaxation exercises, loosening up the muscles, relaxing concentration, breathing exercises—all to help promote recovery.

Evaluation of Training

Planning and evaluation of training constitute a unity. The purpose of evaluation is to check the progress being made in implementing the training plan and to find out how efficient the training methods and means of training are. The use of periodic clinics to check progress enhances the martial artist's overall training. Each check supplies the martial artist valuable information and feedback about their current performance level and abilities. He recognizes his own strengths and weaknesses. Managed properly, the use of such clinics and checks can spur the student on to putting more effort and determination into training.

A Periodic Clinic can be used to evaluate:
1. Basic Fitness
2. Speed/Power
3. Agility
4. Flexibility
5. Awareness
6. On-guard positioning: a. in attack; b. in defense
7. Footwork
8. Attitude
9. Kicking and use of the leg—single/combination
10. Punching and striking—single/combination
11. Techniques—execution; protection; aggressiveness

Continuous familiarization of the martial artist with the effects of the training and its influence on their development of efficiency and long-term conditioning is aimed at enabling the student to train on his own.

\# The basic problem of all martial artist is the "psychical stoppage", where the mind attaches itself to thoughts or any object it encounters. In everyday life his mind is flowing from one object to another. However, when he faces an opponent, his mind is "stopped" and he ceases to be master of himself. Unless the opposition of self and opponent is to be transcended, he is not capable of infinite movements.

Personal handwritten notes by Bruce Lee.

Technique

Technique can be defined as "the mechanical or formal part of an art." The development of technical skills and abilities requires regular practice, attention and concentration, plus constant correction and refinement. Technique is to teach you coordination and proper body mechanics, but should not end there. The natural development of techniques will lead to the loss of conscious awareness after the individual motions have been learned so that the execution in practice or sparring becomes second nature. The idea is not to look for absolute flawless technique, but rather technique which is simple, mechanically sound, and individually suited to that martial artist. In the learning of motor skills there are three characteristic phases. They are:

1. Developing a rough coordination; learning the motor action.
2. Developing a refined coordination; perfecting the motor action.
3. Stabilizing the refined coordination and developing its availability in varying circumstances; stabilizing the motor action.

Mental Training and Attitude

The mental aspects of training are another essential ingredient in Jun Fan martial arts. This is why training methods are utilized which combine physical preparation (tool development, overall conditioning) with psychological preparation (willpower, perseverance, etc.).

Throughout training the student should be trained to act with deliberation, self-reliance, skill and perseverance in coping with training tasks. Mental concentration is required to attain optimum development. Too many students work out without being prepared both mentally and physically. It should be impressed upon every beginner to develop keen observation skills and to mentally register a particular opponent's reactions under specific circumstances.

Developing Mental Attitude Through Sparring

In the course of training, situations similar to combat can be simulated. However, these situations can only appropriate a real situation. In a real fight the available energy sources are often more quickly exhausted than during training. One's fighting experience, emotional and physical states all enter into it.

Only in sparring is it possible to develop to the full the ability to compete to the best advantage against an opponent, to exhaust your strength and energy reserves with maximum economy and sense of purpose, and to master the inner excitement and "surpass oneself." Above all, the mental qualities specific to fighting can only become evident in difficult sparring sessions. For this reason it is necessary for the martial artist to gain plenty of sparring experience, and to also spar against unknown opponents. If you just spar against opponents who are known to you, you may develop stereotyped responses which may cause you trouble when you meet something unusual or unexpected. By participating against varied opponents the martial artist develops the ability to adapt quickly to different conditions. The following are sparring variations which offer variety in training and force the student to adapt to different circumstances:

Progressive Sparring Drills

1. Lead jab only (both people)
2. Front hand only (both people)
3. Lead hand and foot vs. lead hand and foot
4. Lead hand and foot vs. all hands only
5. Lead hand and foot vs. all feet only
6. Lead hand and foot vs. both hands and both feet
7. Lead jab only vs. rear cross only
8. Both hands vs. both hands
9. Both hands vs. both feet
10. Both hands vs. both hands and lead foot
11. Both hands vs. both hands and both feet
12. Both hands vs. lead foot only
13. Both hands/lead foot vs. both hands/lead foot
14. Both hands/lead foot vs. both feet only
15. Both hands/lead foot vs. both hands/both feet
16. Both hands/both feet vs. both hands/both feet
17. Add knees and elbows
18. Add takedowns and throws
19. Add ground fighting
20. Kickboxing vs. grappling
21. Boxing vs. grappling

Environmental Sparring Drills
1. One man standing vs. one man on ground
2. Both people on ground

Note: These are usually short rounds (15-30 seconds)

3. Two people vs. one person
4. Two people vs. three people
5. Two people vs. four people

Note: These are also usually short rounds (15-30 seconds)

6. Line drill—Aggressive person cannot cross line, timid person must cross line and attack.

7. One person stands in circle—any of several surrounding people can attack.

8. Alley training—Lines are drawn to simulate an alley in which two people are attacked by four people. The objective is for the two people to fight their way out of the alley.

Use of Equipment in Training

A wide variety of training equipment is used in Jun Fan. Some can be used by a martial artist alone; others require a training partner. The use of such equipment allows us to cover the entire spectrum of training, and when combined with proper use of the imagination avoids boredom in training and increases the student's skills. Some of the more well-known training devices are:

1. Mook Jong (Wing Cun Dummy)—Enables us to work on trapping skills and power in trapping.
2. Heavy Bag—Good for developing timing and to develop power in striking.
3. Wall Bag—Develops penetration in your punches.
4. Top and Bottom Bag—Valuable for developing distance, timing, footwork and accuracy. Also aids in teaching alertness and recovery.
5. Thai Pads—Developing kicking, kneeing, elbowing speed and power, and building high levels of endurance.
6. Focus Gloves—Builds accuracy and timing in striking, plus timing and distance for speed and power.
7. Kicking Shield—Used to develop "suddenness" in moving, teaches proper distance and penetration.
8. Paper Target—Teaches speed, proper body application, and precise distance.

This 'non-slipping' mind is known as the fluidity, which is also known as the "empty-mind" or 'everyday mind'. To have something in mind means that it is preoccupied and has no time for anything else. But to attempt to remove the thought already in it is to refill it with another something. So what to do? Do nothing! Don't solve it, dissolve it ---- no fuss, no fuss --- it's the everyday mind, nothing special at all. However, if he has any idea at all of displaying his art well, he ceases to be a good martial artist, for his mind 'stops' with every movement he goes through. In all things, it is important to forget your 'mind' and become one with the work at hand.

Personal handwritten notes by Bruce Lee.

Some of the newer pieces of equipment being used are such items as:

1. The Impax Focus Glove. Used to measure both power and reaction speed.

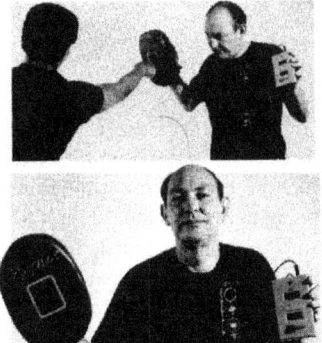

2. The Roto-Bar. Excellent for developing extensor muscles and allowing complete range of movements in weight training.

The Use of Safety Equipment

The use of safety equipment serves several purposes—the primary one being that of reducing the chances of injuries while training hard. Injuries can slow down or even halt your training altogether, thereby impairing your learning. We must differentiate here between the occasional bruise or soreness that accompanies the physicalness of martial arts and the injury such as a torn muscle, strained ligament, or even a broken bone. A certain amount is bound to occur, but you don't need to have your nose broken or knee dislocated in order to know that you've taken a good shot. That mentality is medieval and dangerous. Certain safety equipment can be used which will allow you to make harder contact and yet at the same time keep injuries to a minimum. Equipment such as: headgear; body armor; shin/knee guards; mouthpiece; groin protector (men); chest protector (women).

The amount of protective equipment worn can vary according to the intensity of the training. For basic sparring all one really needs is a mouthpiece and groin or chest protector. One must differentiate between training for competition and training to understand combat. Protective equipment allows you to experience a more "all-out" session and still be in the position of being able to train the following day.

Basic Points of Conditioning

The following are 16 basic points of conditioning which should be developed in the course of training in Jun Fan:

1. Agility
2. Awareness
3. Balance
4. Coordination
5. Flexibility
6. Grace
7. Muscular Development
8. Power
9. Reaction
10. Rhythm
11. Skill
12. Speed
13. Strength
14. Timing
15. General Fitness
16. Technical Knowledge

COMPREHENDING THE TRUE NATURE OF JKD

What is Jeet Kune Do?

This question has echoed through the martial arts world since shortly after Bruce Lee's untimely passing. Why? Because it's an incontrovertible fact that there is no "universally" accepted definition of Jeet Kune Do. If you ask five different people you stand a good chance of getting five different answers. It all depends who you're talking to. This is one of the prime reasons numerous and continuous misperceptions exist today with regard to the art.

Some say, "Jeet Kune Do is Bruce Lee's martial art." That's merely a statement, not a definition. Others say "It's Bruce Lee's own personal expression of martial art." This is even more confusing, because if such is the case, the statement itself declares that no one else could do JKD except Bruce Lee himself. And referring to JKD an "idea" or a "concept" is nebulous and does nothing to help an individual truly understand the art.

Having said this, I cautiously offer the reader my personal definition of Jeet Kune Do, based upon my five decades of being deeply immersed in the art. Jeet Kune Do is "a principle-centered training process to cultivate the ability to express the human body in combative form without any restriction or confinement." It may sound complicated to some, but actually it's very simple. Jeet Kune Do is about

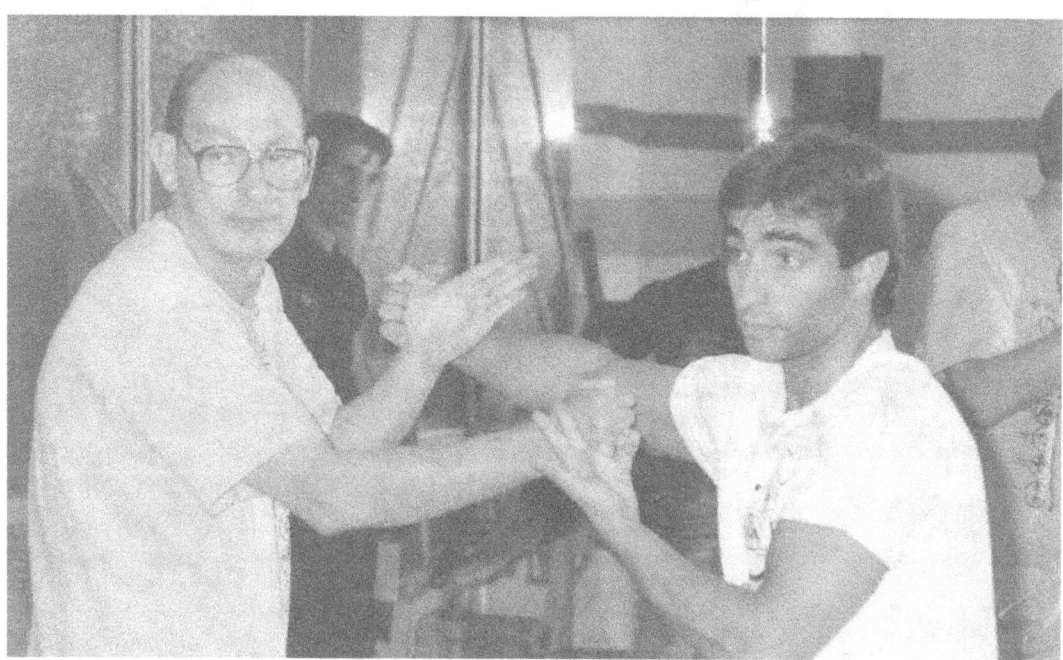

cultivating your body as a martial 'instrument' and expressing yourself with the highest degree of efficiency and effectiveness in combat.

Bruce Lee -- The True 'Root'

With regard to martial arts as a whole, in his personal notes, Bruce Lee wrote, "When you understand the root, you understand all of its blossoming." To comprehend the true nature of Jeet Kune Do, one has to first understand the "root" of the art. The root of Jeet Kune Do was not, as many believe, Wing Chun Gung Fu. While Wing Chun may have served as a launching platform for Lee's martial endeavors, it was merely the first martial art Lee studied in depth. The true "root" of Jeet Kune Do was Bruce Lee himself.

First off, Bruce Lee was a dedicated thinker. It was Lee's mind and his thought processes that allowed him to actualize his potential as a martial artist. It was his mindset and way of thinking that directed him to search for the fundamental truth or "essence" underlying efficient human movement in combat. And when he did, he looked to science rather than tradition, to "motion" rather than "style"; researching human anatomy, physiology, kinesiology and physics. The bottom line was that Bruce Lee was interested in what made for a more efficient kick or punch, not where it came from. And if he absorbed something into his structure, it simply became a part of his personal combative arsenal.

Second, Bruce Lee was a diligent trainer who possessed an incredible work ethic. He understood that to fully actualize his potential and express himself as a martial artist entailed not only cultivating his mind to be fluid, receptive, and nonrestrictive, but also cultivating his body into what he called a 'martial instrument,' and developing the ability to express himself with that instrument to its highest degree. He was not a casual enthusiast who would train a couple of times a week for a few hours, or go an hour and a half a week to this martial art class and then study another martial art for an hour two times a week. Lee spent thousands of hours training, researching and investigating martial arts, fitness, psychology, and philosophy.

In addition, Bruce Lee was not simply "open-minded", meaning that he would take in everything without any type of analysis. Rather, he applied critical-thinking to what he did and was willing to put forth the hours necessary to research and perfect whatever he was working on. What it boils down to is that Bruce Lee did the work. And the work was intended for himself, not anyone else. Lee was concerned with his own personal development. He wasn't being selfish, he was being realistic.

Finally, for anyone involved in JKD, to truly understand Lee's ultimate view regarding martial arts and JKD's trajectory of development one needs to follow his personal evolution as a martial artist all the way through his life, past the time when he initially conceived of the idea of the "ultimate" gung fu system, beyond the time when he christened what he was doing "Jeet Kune Do, all the way up to when, shortly before his passing away, he was throwing things away and getting rid of the idea of "styles" and "methods" altogether.

It's About "Totality"

Jeet Kune Do is and always has been about totality of one's combative tools and complete freedom in using them. Tim and I are both fortunate to have in our possession copies of Bruce Lee's 7 volume "Commentaries on the Martial Way" (both original and typed versions), which were given to us by both Dan Inosanto and Linda Lee Cadwell. The following are some notes which are taken directly from Volume 7. This particular volume was laid out more as a personal training journal as compared to the others, which were more notes drawn from various sources. For this reason at the top of a page you will see written such things as "Research Notes for November 12 (Thurs.) 1970" --

All-in fighting does not replace any known system of close fighting, nor does it evolve about any single style of defense and counter-attack. It makes use of all known forms of personal combat, and any other means that will accomplish a quick kill.
- Good conditioning and athletic ability
- Scientific training of a boxer -- fine coordination, sense of timing and distance
- Sophistication of a fencer
- Attitude and mental development of Zen, Taoism, etc.

Specialized All-in Fighting
1) poking eyes
2) pulling hair -- as immobilization, as release, as assist
3) biting -- as release to disable and to attack in close
4) practice forearm pinching to hurt
5) grabbing groin
6) specialize in under belt attack with kicks, strikes, punches, and grappling

Let "body feel" on the forearm as a destructive weapon (use as loose club snap or club) alongside with elbowing.

Look into breaking the joint and limbs:
breaking by
a) directed kicking -- thrust kick, push thrust, snap kick
b) directed striking
c) limb locks by pressure

Practice relaying inverted bottom fist to groin or "downed" opponent alongside

Practice relaying snapping forearm smash -- add to tools possibility

Investigate into butting:-
1) with head
2) with hips and buttocks
3) with shoulder

Investigate --
a) elbowing
b) kneeing

Investigate into fighting from
1) as attack into opponent
2) as counter
3) using legs mainly
4) using legs and hand
(develop such mastery that one can fight safely from the ground)

Investigate into clawing with attempt to tear apart the
a) throat
b) groin
c) hair

Investigate into hand hook to pull opponent down backward

How can I be a master fighter?
obtain "direct body feel" of devastating:-
a) throwing
b) left side kicking and punching
c) ground fighting
d) hara in changes

Again, in Lee's notes in Commentaries on the Martial Way,
In another one of the volumes, Lee noted:

The importance of fluidity in interchanging of:
1) Hitting/kicking
2) Grappling/throwing
3) Joint locks

a) standing
b) on the ground
c) immobilizing techniques for -- (1) arms (2) legs

Getting Rid of "Styles" and "Labels"

Let's deal with the issue of "styles" as they relate to Jeet Kune Do. The fact that Bruce Lee was interested in the root of efficient human movement in combat meant that there was nothing that he excluded or opposed, except for styles.

Sometimes, when I see a person observing an individual training in JKD, I hear them make comments such as, "Oh, he's doing Wing Chun" -- "He's doing Thai Boxing" -- "He's doing Brazilian Jiu Jitsu", etc. But the fact is that they aren't. They're expressing themselves by punching, or trapping, grappling, or whatever. This can be likened to someone listening to a musician play a piece of music and saying, "Now he's playing Mozart classical, now he's playing Winton Marsalis jazz, now he's doing Mick Jagger rock." Or watching a dancer performing on stage and saying, "Oh now she's doing ballet, now she's doing jazz, now she's doing hip-hop." At the other end of the spectrum is the individual who watches someone training in JKD and says, "Now they're doing a JKD kick, now they're doing a JKD punch, etc. Again, this is incorrect. The individual is simply expressing themselves using whatever technique or action they use at the moment. The problem is that the people making these types of statements (even the person using "JKD kick") are still hung up on "styles" and categorizing or labeling what they see as being from "this" style or "that" style,even down to the current label du jour, "He's doing MMA."

While Bruce Lee drew what he referred as "essences" from diverse forms of combat, both Eastern and Western (and although certain techniques or actions were included,many times these essences were such things as speed, power, economy of motion, etc.), he did not keep the names of the sources attached to what he was doing. He didn't, for example, tell his students, "Okay, now we're do this punch, which comes from Western boxing" or "Now we're going to do this footwork, which comes from Western Fencing" or "Alright, let's work on this hand immobilization that comes from Wing Chun Gung Fu."

If one takes the time and puts forth the energy to read any of Lee's written material, or listen to any of his written, audio and video interviews, they will get a very clear understanding of what Lee's view was concerning the idea or notion of "styles." At the time preceding his death, Lee viewed styles as "cages" or "chains."

One of the fundamental underlying principles in JKD is about moving beyond separations of styles and instead simply looking at martial art in terms of motion, of efficient human movement. When I began training in JKD, one of the first things Sifu Dan Inosanto kept reaffirming to me was, "Chris, if you understand motion, you don't need 'style."

It's All About YOU

If you are a practitioner of Jeet Kune Do, remember this, JKD is not about the perpetuation of a style, but rather the personal cultivation of an individual as a martial artist. JKD is about YOU. It's not

about learning this style and that style or combining bits from different styles, but rather, it's cultivating your own body as a martial instrument and then expressing that instrument with the highest degree of efficiency and effectiveness. You have to investigate and learn about yourself; your abilities, your reactions, your prejudices, your attributes. You have to develop body awareness and self-awareness. You have to know what you can do. Not what technique you can use if the opponent does this or that, but what your body is capable of doing, and how to enter the proper mindset and relate to the opponent.

Finally, Jeet Kune Do is a problem-solving art, and each individual must do the problem-solving for themselves. If you do not actively participate in the process, you will never understand JKD. You cannot simply go into the school or training facility and expect the teacher to give it to you, no matter how good the teacher. Bruce Lee did the work himself, and so must each individual who is training in Jeet Kune Do. You have to do the work. Serious work, not just a casual, "I go to class two times a week for an hour each time and then do nothing else" kind of work. If you are willing to do the work, put forth the time and energy, develop the proper mental attitude, and establish a clear perspective concerning what JKD is all about, you will be able say with confidence, "I understand the true nature of Jeet Kune Do."

THE JKD "TRAINING PYRAMID"

While Bruce Lee believed that there should be no such thing as a "fixed" system or method of fighting, he did however, firmly believe that there is a definite progressive approach to training. In my years of training in and teaching JKD, I've come to view this progressive approach to training in the form of a pyramid. The shape itself is not really important. What is important is how the overall structure fits together into a unified and cohesive whole.

The pyramid is divided into eight layers or levels. The base, or **Level 1** of the pyramid is comprised of the on-guard or ready position along with footwork and mobility skills.

Level 2 is tool development; learning how to use all of one's various weapons (hands, feet, elbows, knees, forearms, etc.) with speed, power and precision.

Level 3 deals with developing one's offensive or attacking skills. This includes not only striking, but also such grappling skills as joint-locking, throwing, choking, and hand immobilization skills.

Level 4 is comprised of counter-offensive and defensive skills. This would include counterattack skills such as interception or stop-hitting, evasion--and-counter, parry-and-counter, along with developing good defensive abilities.

Level 5 deals with developing one's timing and rhythm abilities as well as a good understanding of various distances.

Developing essential qualities such as speed, power and endurance to enhance your martial art performance follows in **Level 6**.

Level 7 focuses upon fighting tactics and strategies.

Level 8, the peak of the pyramid is all-out sparring, in which all of the other levels are put together and used. This level is about getting as close to real combat as is possible.

It's important to understand that the pyramid I use is merely a way of looking at the overall training structure, and the various elements are separated merely for convenience sake. It does not mean that a person has to complete or master one level before they can move on to the next, because in reality all of the various elements are interrelated and linked together. However, if a martial artist leaves out various sections of the pyramid, or uses poor-quality materials in constructing it, they will likely end up with a structure that is very shaky and not very dependable. Think about it for a moment. How can a fighter concentrate on using tactics if they cannot rely on their footwork and mobility skills, or if they are unsure about the quality of their weapons? So, however you choose to view training in JKD, make sure it covers all of the elements discussed above.

Keep Training Well!

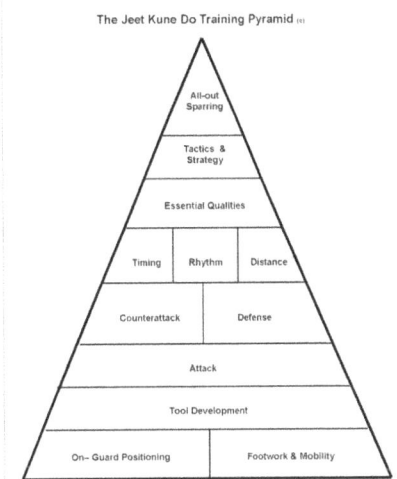

GLOSSARY OF JUN FAN TERMINOLOGY

1. Kwoon — school, gym, institute
2. Si-jo — Founder of the style, system, method
3. Si-fu — Instructor/Teacher
4. Si-hing — your senior, your older brother
5. Si-bak — Instructor's senior (uncle)
6. Si-sook — Instructor's junior (uncle)
7. Si-gung — your instructor's Instructor (grandfather)
8. Si-dai — your junior, your younger brother
9. Toe-dai — student
10. Toe-suen — student's student
11. Joap Hop — group together
12. Yu Bay! — ready!
13. Gin Lai — salute, salutation
14. Hay, Hey — begin
15. Bai Jong — ready position
16. Ha Da — low hit
17. Jung Da — middle hit
18. Go Da — high hit
19. Biu Jee — finger jab
20. Ch'ung chuie — vertical fist
21. Gua chuie — back fist
22. Ping chuie — horizontal fist
23. Choap chuie — knuckle fist
24. O'ou chuie — hooking fist
25. Jik Ch'ung — straight blast
26. Pak sao — slapping hand
27. Lop sao — grabbing hand
28. Jut sao — jerking hand
29. Jao sao — running hand
30. Huen sao — circling hand
31. Tan sao — palm up block
32. Mon sao — inquisitive hand
33. Wu sao — protecting hand
34. Fook sao — bent arm elbow in block
35. Boang sao — raised elbow deflection
36. Doan chi — single sticking hand
37. Chi sao — sticking hands
38. Phon sao — trapping hands
39. Sut — knee
40. Jang — elbow
41. Jeet Tek — stop kick, intercepting kick
42. Jik tek — straight kick
43. Juk tek — side kick
44. O'ou tek — hook kick, roundhouse kick
45. Hou tek — back kick
46. Juen tek — spin kick
47. So tek — sweeping kick
48. Dum tek — stomp kick
49. Ha so tek — inverted sweep kick
50. Gua tek — inverted hook kick
51. Goang sao — low outer wrist block
52. Ha pak — low slap cover
53. Woang pak — cross hand slap cover

Art lives where absolute freedom is, because where it is not, there can be no creativity — — — has no ego rigidity.

The ultimate goal of discipline in ~~the martial art~~ J.K.D. is where learning gained is learning lost.

Personal handwritten notes by Bruce Lee.

168

APPENDIX

BIBLIOGRAPHY

1. L. Matveyev. *Fundamentals of Sports Training*, Progress Publishers (1981).
2. *Principles of Sports Training*, Sportsverlag Publications (1982).
3. H. DeVries. *Physiology of Exercise*, Wm. Brown Co. (1974).
4. Michel Alaux. *Modern Fencing*, Charles Scribner's Sons (1975).
5. C.L. De Beaumont. *Fencing—Ancient Art and Modern Sport*, A.S. Barnes and Co. (1970).
6. U.S. Navy. *Boxing*, U.S. Naval Institute (1943).
7. Bruce Lee. *Tao of Jeet Kune Do*, Ohara Publications (1975).
8. M. Yessis/F. Hatfield. *Plyometrics—Achieving Explosive Power in Sports*, Fitness Systems (1986).
9. J. Robinson. *Sports Research Monthly*, American Sports Research Association.
10. C. Kent/T. Tackett. *Jeet Kune Do Kickboxing*, Know Now Publishing (1986).

SPECIAL TRAINING EQUIPMENT

IMPAX Focus Glove available from:
    Impulse Sports Training Systems Inc.
    30612 Salem Drive
    Bay Village, Ohio 44140

ROTO-BAR available from:
    Exerquipment Inc.
    616 Enterprise Drive
    Oak Brook, Illinois 60521

Additional photographs were shot at:
    Magda Institute of Martial Arts
    7255 Canby Avenue
    Reseda, Ca. 91335
    (818) 342-2455

JEET KUNE DO: GUIDE TO EQUIPMENT TRAINING
By Chris Kent

"MAXIMIZE YOUR FIGHTING SKILLS"
Regardless of what styles or methods of martial arts you train in, "Jeet Kune Do: Guide to Equipment Training" offers comprehensive and cohesive training information that will help you maximize your combat skills and achieve your full potential as a martial artist and fighter. Detailed and progressive instruction on how to use the heavy bag, focus mitts, forearm pad, kicking shield, etc... makes this book the main source of information about the proper use of equipment training. This book will take you to a new level of integration and mastery of your art, regardless of the style, if what you are interested in is real contact power!

US $45.00 – 7 x 10 – 350 pages approx.

FOR PURCHASE VISIT:
WWW. MARTIALARTSDIGITAL.COM

ENCYCLOPEDIA OF JEET KUNE DO - A to Z
By Chris Kent

Jeet Kune Do is the art of expressing the human body in combative form. It is not a "style" or "system" of martial art as conventionally defined. Nor is it simply an eclectic conglomeration of fighting techniques from various arts combined with philosophical dogma that is convenient. Jeet Kune Do is a rational, well thought-out approach to "total" martial art training.
The "Encyclopedia of Jeet Kune Do" is designed to serve as a resource guide, not only for the person training in Jeet Kune Do, but for any martial artist sincerely interested in enhancing his or her performance and achieving one's full potential.
Many of the principles and training methods illustrated in one section or chapter of this book can and should be cross-referenced with motions or actions in another. The goal is for you, the reader, to use this book to improve your understanding and working knowledge of the art, science, and philosophy of unarmed combat known as Jeet Kune Do. Remember, it's not how much you absorb, but how much of what you've absorbed that you can apply "alively" that counts.

US $34.95 – 7 x 10 – 350 pages approx.

FOR PURCHASE VISIT:
WWW. MARTIALARTSDIGITAL.COM

ESSENTIAL JEET KUNE DO
The Way of Intercepting Fist
By Tim Tackett

This book will serve way to decide what will work the best for you and what aspects of JKD you need to keep, as well as throw away. I feel that it would be impossible to learn this from your instructor, as he will mainly focus on what works best for him. I have been fortunate to have learned from many of the senior students of Bruce Lee and have noticed that they all focus on certain things and not on what some the others are doing. For some it may be the boxing aspects. For some it may be footwork. For others it was trapping energy and the Wing Chun elements. It was only when we started focusing on the Western fencing aspects of JKD that I was able to understand and focus on what has become my essence of JKD. Of course, an instructor cannot just hand you what will become your essence or foundation of your own JKD. This is something that you must discover for yourself as you work to become more a more efficient JKD practitioner. The purpose of this book is too show you most of what we teach in my garage and the basic principles behind each. Once you have worked on these you will come to realize what will work for you and what will not. Some of you will want to focus on distance and footwork. Others will feel comfortable crashing the line. Whatever works for you is the main thing. Just use the book as guideline to discover your own essential JKD.

US $45.00 – 7 x 10 – 350 pages approx.

FOR PURCHASE VISIT:
WWW. MARTIALARTSDIGITAL.COM

JEET KUNE DO PRINCIPLES
For All Martial Artist
By Tim Tackett

The title of this book is "Jeet Kune Do Principles". Principles and concepts that ALL Martial Artists – regardless of style - can use in their daily training. In fact, most of these principles are used everyday by all martial artists around the world, and most like speed and timing, are not unique to the art of Jeet Kune Do. The purpose of this book is to explain some of these principles and share some ideas on how to train for them. Some are principles like the use of distance and broken rhythm in combat, while others are sayings on combat by the founder of JKD Bruce Lee that perfectly illustrate a principle or a fighting idea. To understand the root, you need to understand the principles.
The principles of Jeet Kune Do are universal, but unfortunately these principles are no longer stressed as much anymore, because there is too much focus on "technique" alone, and seeing how many techniques you can "add" to your toolbox.
The purpose of this work is to discuss some of the principles that the art of JKD focuses on, and to give you some examples to put those principles in action. The hope of this book is that you do the same with the main techniques you either are studying or teaching – regardless of your style.

US $45.00 – 7 x 10 – 350 pages approx.

FOR PURCHASE VISIT:
WWW. MARTIALARTSDIGITAL.COM

www.ingramcontent.com/pod-product-compliance
Lightning Source LLC
Chambersburg PA
CBHW081448070526
44586CB00019B/2266